DIGITAL COSTUME DESIGN AND COLLABORATION

Digital Costume Design and Collaboration gives in-depth instruction on how to draw, render, and fully design costumes using online tools and software. Grounded in the use of Photoshop, the book explains the process of building a costume design from scratch, including information on digital tools and painting techniques. The book demonstrates how to utilize social media, such as Flickr and Pinterest, to compile research; how to create user-friendly Web-based slide shows; and how to archive digital files for portfolios and personal websites. It also demonstrates how to organize spec sheets, plots, and inventories using Google Docs for easy editing and Dropbox for easy file sharing. A companion YouTube channel featuring video tutorials of exercises and applications complements the book.

Rafael Jaen is a practicing costume designer, professor, and author. Jaen's costume design (and manufacturing) work includes film, TV, and theatre, and he has received multiple accolades and award nominations including the prestigious Elliot Norton Award and the IRNE Award. He has been a member of the United States Institute for Theatre Technology (USITT), the United Scenic Artist (USA) 829, and the National Association of Photoshop Professionals (NAPP). He has served at the USITT Board of Directors and on the Publications Committee. Jaen has also served as National Design, Technology, and Management Chair for the Kennedy Center American College Theater Festival (KCACTF), and he serves as the USITT–KCACTF Communications Liaison. Jaen is an Associate Professor of Costume Design at UMASS Boston, MA.

RAFAEL JAEN

DIGITAL COSTUME DESIGN AND COLLABORATION

APPLICATIONS *IN ACADEMIA, THEATRE, AND FILM*

Routledge
Taylor & Francis Group

NEW YORK AND LONDON

First published 2018
by Routledge
711 Third Avenue, New York, NY 10017

and by Routledge
2 Park Square, Milton Park, Abingdon, Oxon OX14 4RN

Routledge is an imprint of the Taylor & Francis Group, an informa business

© 2018 Taylor & Francis

Library of Congress Cataloging in Publication Data

Names: Jaen, Rafael, author.
Title: Digital costume design and collaboration : applications in academia, theatre, and film / Rafael Jaen.
Description: New York : Routledge, Taylor & Francis Group, 2017. | Includes bibliographical references and index.
Identifiers: LCCN 2016053621| ISBN 9781138935730 (hbk : alk. paper) | ISBN 9781138935723 (pbk : alk. paper) | ISBN 9781315677200 (ebk)
Subjects: LCSH: Costume design—Data processing. | Clothing and dress—Computer-aided design.
Classification: LCC PN2067 .J34 2017 | DDC 792.02/6—dc23

ISBN: 978-1-138-93573-0 (hbk)
ISBN: 978-1-138-93572-3 (pbk)
ISBN: 978-1-315-67720-0 (ebk)

Typeset in Avenir and DIN
by Keystroke, Neville Lodge, Tettenhall, Wolverhampton

Visit the companion YouTube channel: www.youtube.com/user/JaenRafael/videos

Printed and bound in India by Replika Press Pvt. Ltd.

TO THE MANY STUDENTS, COLLEAGUES, FAMILY, AND FRIENDS ACROSS THE USA AND OVERSEAS WHO HAVE INSPIRED ME THROUGHOUT MY CAREER JOURNEY. I SHARE THIS ACHIEVEMENT WITH YOU!

Especial thanks to my spouse Stephen Brady, my student collaborators Colleen Fitzgibbons and Ben Sibley, and the editors at Routledge. Your constant support and contributions fueled my journey.

ACKNOWLEDGMENTS

As a practicing 21st-century designer, I find that it is important to combine one's classical training with the use of digital applications. I regularly combine Flickr archives, Pinterest, Google Docs, iPhone apps, etc. to help tackle the design process "on the go." This saves time, and alleviates the competing demands in today's work field. I've also focused on producing sketches using Photoshop. I save them as PDF files and email them without using scanners, printers, watercolor paper, etc. This software allows me to translate basic principles of traditional media—such as watercolor transparency and acrylic opacity—into digital renderings full of substance and intent. In addition, the engineering behind it provides me with a painting desk-station that I can use anywhere; making fast design changes with no fuss. Photoshop has become pivotal in my digital approach to costume design.

With this book, I intend to help the readers discover their favorite Photoshop tools, modalities, and effects, helping them actualize their ideas. Through various chapters and tutorials, I will translate the complete design process into a digital platform while following the more traditional "true and tried" methodology. For example, when looking at script analysis we'll refer to human geography principles and other "givens" by answering questions such as:

1. What does the script mention that addresses the character's costumes and mannerisms?

2. What are the character's underlining motivations, back-story, and secrets or the character's "spine"?

3. What aspects of the script are relevant to the character's storyline or development arch, and does the historical period or other given plot point impact the character?

4. What are the emotions, qualities, and actions that are part of the character's core?

I have been fortunate enough to present my findings at various USITT Professional Development Workshops (PDWs), at Costume Symposiums, and at various colleges around the country. I have also taught online courses on this subject. My goal now is to reach a larger audience by sharing my process in this book. By the end of it, the reader will be able to create digital archives that include research, finished sketches, costume specs, fitting photos, and beautiful portfolio-ready images to share with production teams and feature on their website.

Let's design, paint, and organize on the go with no fuss!

Rafael

In the article "An Unforgettable Affair with Photoshop", costume designer Esther Van Eek wrote:

The standing ovation at the end of the third day said it all. . . . There was a triumphant atmosphere in the classroom on the last day, when Mr. Jaen had each person share a rendering showing what had been learned. Any misgivings that digital rendering might cause designers to lose their individuality disappeared during this final presentation.[1]

I have been fortunate enough to present my digital approach at various Professional Development Workshops (PDWs), and costume symposiums, and at multiple colleges around the USA. I have also taught successful online courses.

The tools in Photoshop have allowed me to create digital costume renderings, using multiple B & W (black & white outline) silhouette layers, and then "flatting" them. This is a technique that I have taught via online classes, and YouTube videos.

Digital Costume Design and Collaboration contains various chapters, with tutorials that will assist the reader in translating the complete design process into a Web-sharing platform. I follow "true and tried" methodology. From script analysis to talking to directors and actors; from producing research plates to rendering beautiful and effective sketches; and from creating a digital costume bible to updating individual Web pages. With each step, I describe the type of software and applications that work best, and ways to use Web sharing—avoiding superfluous printing—and end with a greener approach. By the end of it, the reader will be able to create Web archives to share with production teams, and feature on their professional website.

Join me in rediscovering the excitement and passion that motivate costume designers. Let's get inspired and try all or some of my digital approaches.

Let's share a standing ovation!

Rafael

Note

1   Esther Van Eek. "An Unforgettable Affair With Photoshop." USITT Sightlines. Costume Design & Technology Commission. October 2011. Accessed July 15, 2015. http://sightlines.usitt.org/archive/2011/10/CostumeSymposium.asp.

IT IS IMPORTANT THAT THE DESIGNERS KNOW HOW NECESSARY THEY ARE
TO THE PROCESS AND THAT IF THEY TRUST THE PLAY AND OUR PROCESS
TOGETHER, THAT WE WILL LIKELY MAKE ONE OF THE MOST AUTHENTIC,
MEMORABLE AND MOVING PIECES OF THEATER IN ANY GIVEN SEASON.

SHAWN LACOUNT, ARTISTIC DIRECTOR AND DIRECTOR[1]

THE DESIGN PROCESS: A DIGITAL APPROACH

For me, the costume design process starts when I read the script for the first time. I like to pay close attention to the response that it elicits in me, keeping track of the ideas or themes that may come to mind. I usually start by defining the character's "spine," meaning the core emotions, qualities, and actions. This is the cardinal point of the process, and it helps when talking to a director. After a second reading, I put these emotions, qualities, and actions into one or two words, and then I translate them into visual language. The idea is to get into the storyline, finding the things that are compelling to me. For example, I may use a character's journey from "repressed" to "liberated" as my design arc, following their gradual transformation from beginning to end and from one type of person to another, starting with tightly buttoned-up clothing and severe colors, and moving to looser fabrics and relaxed styles later in the story. Another sample would be someone who has a "sparkling" personality or who is in a musical number that is "effervescent." These words could easily facilitate the translation of the characters' visual traits into textures in the fabrics and/or accessories. Finally, there may be a fast-paced scene with lots of "hustle and bustle"; the busy and noisy activity could inspire me to explore multi-layered garments that would add to the movement and give a sense of the energy and excitement I felt when reading the script.

In this chapter, I will use as a sample my design work for *Edith Can Shoot Things and Hit Them*. This was a New England premiere by A. Rey Pamatmat, directed by Shawn LaCount and co-produced by Company One and the Huntington Theatre, in Boston, MA, in June 2015.

Their website synopsis states:

With no parents, little food, and nothing in the bank account, 12-year-old Edith, her brother Kenny, and a giant stuffed frog are doing just fine, thank you very much. Making the rules up as they go, Kenny gets more than mix-tapes from his new friend, Benji, and Edith ends up shooting

something for real. Funny and full of heart, this coming of age story explores the gap between childhood and whatever comes next.[2]

The characters included Edith, a 12-year-old Filipino-American girl, and Kenny, her 16-year-old brother. There is also Benji (his best friend), described as a young man of any race, and who is 16 as well. The action takes place in the early nineties on a non-working farm outside of the remotest town in Middle America.

First Reactions

The following email conversation with Peter Meacham, an Educational Associate of Company One Theatre, in Boston, MA, illustrates my first reactions to this play. He interviewed me on May 28, 2015 for *Curricular Connections*, an instructional packet and study guide dedicated to student audiences and their teachers.

Peter: How would you describe the difference between the internal and external influences on a character's costume? Can you use examples for Edith, Benji, and Kenny?

Rafael: I usually start by defining the character's "spine," meaning the core emotions, qualities, and actions. Edith is feral, yet innocent and playful. Benji is introspected, sheltered, and impulsive. Kenny is watchful, orderly, and scared. Both Edith and Kenny fit the profile of "parentified children" according to Dr. Allan Schwartz, LCSW and PhD's definition.[3] Kenny takes care of dressing his little sister, cleaning the house, preparing meals for the family, and supervising her activities. Having this perspective helps me make choices about his wardrobe; he has to appear more responsible than an average kid.

FIGURE 1.1

Company One banner for *Edith Can Shoot Things and Hit Them.*

Peter: How does the concept of a "character's armor" influence or aid the design process? Can you share examples of Edith, Benji, and Kenny's "armor"?

Rafael: Once I have a sense of the internal world of the characters, and a point of view to help me access their motivations and secrets, I begin to build their imaginary closet [with garments that the characters might wear as they move through their lives in the play]. I address the needs of the script, but I also look for iconic items that will endow the characters with meaning and foreshadow their journey. I call this the "character's armor." One piece of Edith's armor would be her overalls; they give her the ability to roam freely and hang from the barn's rafters. One of Benji's would be his large glasses, and for Kenny, it would be his jean jacket that helps him blend in and disappear in public.

Peter: When deciding on internal and external influences, what design conclusions can you draw from the script, and what must be developed in conversations and in rehearsals with the director, the actors, and the dramaturges? Do you have examples of this from concept meetings and rehearsals?

Rafael: After defining the character's "spine," I move to other parameters referenced in the script. These would include geographical location, time period, season, local traditions, socio-economics, etc. It is always important to discuss them at length with the director, the actors, and the production team so the production has a cohesive look and style. In our show, a really good example [of discussing ideas with the director and design team] is the color palette; I arrived at the idea of using secondary and primary colors with black accents after discussing the comic strip *Shade the Changing Man* with director Shawn LaCount and the team. I am looking at the 1977 illustrations for textures and the 1990 ones for color and graphics.

Peter: What is unique, challenging, or exciting about designing costumes for the 1990s?

Rafael: One singular thing about the 1990s is the use of large textures and complementary colors, as seen on TV shows and popular magazines from the time. There are trends such as the Hello Kitty brand that still remain today. There are other aspects that are real specific but may not have been accessible to our characters. For example, the Calvin Klein briefs made famous by Marky (Wahlberg) Mark. In our show,

I have to keep in mind the geographical location where the characters live, and their socio-economic status. This will influence the final costume choices.

Peter: How is designing for children different than designing for adults?

Rafael: I have to take into account the function of the clothes. If they are everyday clothes, they have to be more durable, resistant, and easy to maintain. If they are school uniforms, they would be color-fast and easy to wash and dry. In our show, the challenge is

that I am designing for adults playing children. So the clothes have to be even sturdier.

Compiling Information Digitally to Create Web-Based Shared Archives

I track all my notes online using Google Docs, Sheets, and Slides (Figure 1.2). This is an easy way to share and discuss key information with directors, costume assistants, and the rest of the production team.

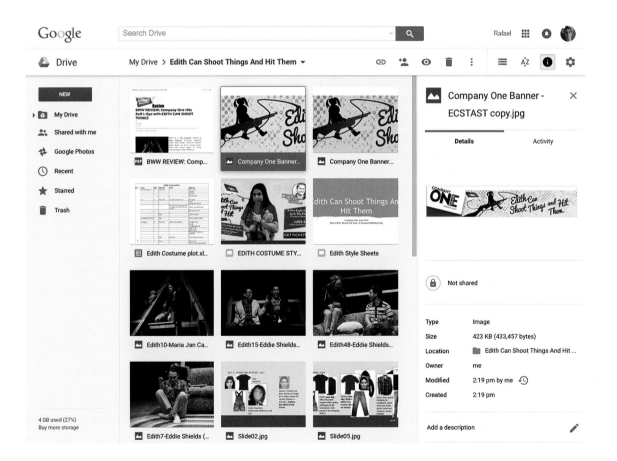

FIGURE 1.2

A Google Folder sample for *Edith Can Shoot Things and Hit Them.*

[These Web-based] productivity apps that let you create different kinds of online documents, work on them in real time with other people, and store them in your Google Drive online—all for free. You can access the documents, spreadsheets, and presentations you create from any computer, anywhere in the world. (There's even some work you can do without an Internet connection! Google Docs is an online word processor that lets you create and format text documents and collaborate with other people in real time. Google Sheets is an online spreadsheet app that lets you create and format spreadsheets and simultaneously work with other people. Google Slides is an online presentations app that allows you to show off your work in a visual way.[4]

I always create Word tables or Excel spreadsheets with all the costume and character-specific references, including the script's page numbers. This is an easy way to share and discuss key information with directors, costume assistants, and the rest of the production team (Figure 1.3).

When talking to a director, I also find that it is necessary to translate my design ideas into visual language. I like to compile my research, and make it available to them and the rest of the production team right away. I want to make sure that we are on the same page, literally seeing the same things. This helps avoid surprises and misunderstandings. I find that Pinterest is the perfect tool for this; it allows me to easily share online pinboards via a link. This online source is driven entirely by visuals, and like every other social media site, it has its own lingo:

1. When you share something on Pinterest, each bookmark is called a pin. An important feature is that you can add Web links to each image to refer to later. I do this when I pin Web journal articles or Kindle books, for example.

2. When you share someone else's pin on Pinterest, it's called a repin. You can search the site by topic and add relevant images easily this way.

3. You can group pins together by topic onto various boards or pinboards in your profile. Each board mimics a real-life pinboard.

An important tool that this application offers is the image "edit" option. After a photo is uploaded to a board, it can be opened, and all sorts of information can be added. I like to include the Web address for future reference; especially if it is an item that I may have to buy! As of July 5, 2015, the *What is Pinterest?—For Dummies* website says: "You can easily upload images onto Pinterest. Using the 'Pin It' button, you can share directly in your browser from any web page. You can also share your pins on Twitter and Facebook." (Figure 1.4)

Working in academia, I have observed that digital language seems to be part of the DNA of the younger generations. I am lucky to always interact with students who are current in social media platforms and new apps. In the next pages, I am sharing the research from a former student. She devised an approach that is very useful both for design work and for scholarly contributions.

A New Look: Updating Research Methods
By Colleen Fitzgibbons

I was approached in January 2015 with an opportunity to co-write an essay that would be part of a Joseph Healy Grant,[5] which Professor Jaen and his students had been working on for various months. This paper created an opportunity for collaboration between mentor and mentee as well as new professional endeavors for all involved. The Grant called for an essay that would better explain the purpose of using a historical figure as a vehicle for teaching and preserving the unique art that is haute couture.

Professor Jaen allowed me to conduct my own research using any and all sources available so I could create

Edith Costume Notes and Inventory

Act:	Scene:	Page:	Character:	Notes	Wearing:
	Everyone Says So	1	Edith		Red stained t-shirt
			12 years old		Jean Overalls
					Barefoot
	Liar	2	Kenny	Dressed to leave home	Blue Polo
			16 years old	fairly average	Jeans
					Jean Jacket
		6	Edith	Same as above	Might put on shoes onstage
	Hunting for Gnomes	7--8	Edith	Same as above	
	Changing	8	Benji	Clothes are starched	Yellow T-shirt
			16 years old		Glasses
					Orange Plaid shirt
					Khaki Pants
					Brown Booties
					Blue jacket
			Edith	New Day	Same as above
			Kenny		Add-On blue hoodie open
1	Interruption	14-17	Kenny	Same as above	Zip up hoodie
			Edith	Same as above	
			Benji	Same as above	Take jacket off on stage
	Science	17-23	Kenny	Different Day	Zips up the hoodie
			Benji	QC ON STAGE	Open plaid shirt -showing yellow t-shirt
	Keeping Watch	23-25	Edith	Change t-shirt	Add-on Black T-shirt
					Add-on Purple Hoodie
					Overalls
			Kenny	Same as above --QC at end of scene	
			Benji	Same as above --QC at end of scene	

By Rafael Jaen   7/21/15   Page 1

FIGURE 1.3

A Google Docs sample table with scene-by-scene costume notes for *Edith Can Shoot Things and Hit Them*. The actual document has a total of four pages, with twenty-nine scenes. It includes script's needs and director's notes.

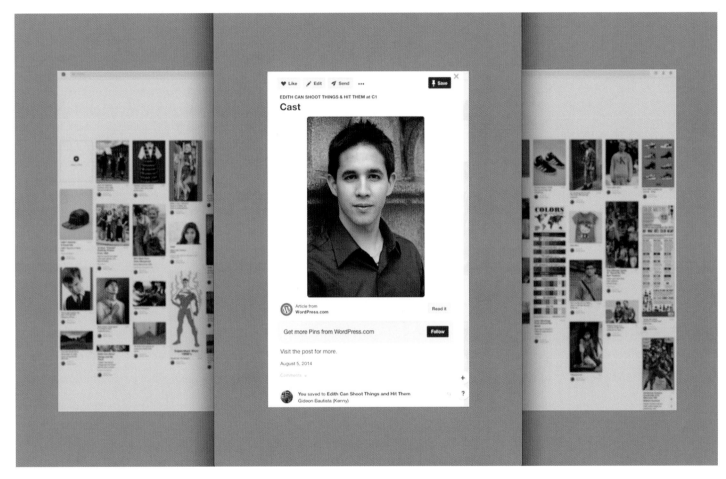

FIGURE 1.4

Detail of an image from my Pinterest page for *Edith Can Shoot Things and Hit Them*. Actor Gideon Bautista played Kenny. I included the headshots of the actors, looking at their skin tone and hair color as part of my color palette.

a historical context for the project; by giving me this freedom, I created a research process that integrates the use of scholarly sources, social media, and collaborative forums to produce work that is both relevant and effective. I was fortunate enough to be able to take this process to the USITT Conference in Cincinnati in Spring 2015 and present among MFA students as part of the Costume Commission Student Leadership Initiatives. This research process can be broken down into six concise steps that are referred to as **The Six Cs**:

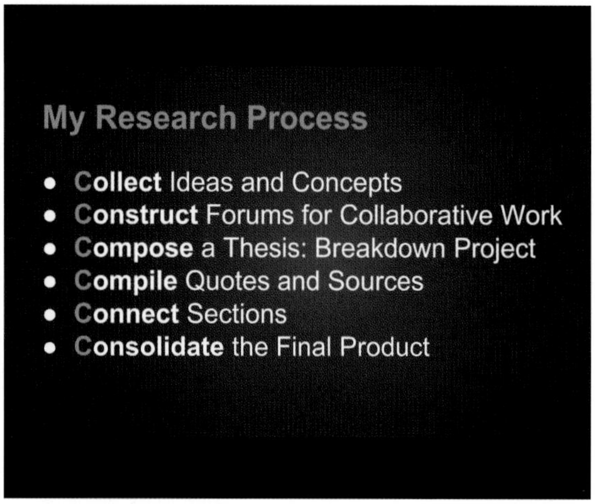

My Research Process

- **C**ollect Ideas and Concepts
- **C**onstruct Forums for Collaborative Work
- **C**ompose a Thesis: Breakdown Project
- **C**ompile Quotes and Sources
- **C**onnect Sections
- **C**onsolidate the Final Product

FIGURE 1.5

The Six Cs.

In order to first collect ideas and concepts, the recommended forum is a website called Pinterest. While this site is a form of social media, it is also a wonderful starting point for research. This website provides images that are often hyper-linked to websites, articles, blogs, etc.; these images may be organized, or "pinned," on various boards which can be kept private or shared with specific people. There is also an option to create collaborative boards where anyone involved in the project

is able to add to and update the existing board. One of the most important features of this site is the ability to "pin" articles and sources found elsewhere to boards so that it may function as a preliminary or working bibliography. This website is both free and user friendly, and therefore a terrific way to integrate research and modern technology.

Pinterest is only one of the collaborative forums in this process; the forum used most prominently throughout the process is Google Docs (see Figure 1.5). Google Docs is an online office that provides templates for Word documents, slideshows, and spreadsheets. These documents are accessible to anyone with an Internet connection and a Gmail account. These documents may be kept private, but are also easily shared with colleagues who will have the ability to edit, read, and make changes at the discretion of the document's creator. Apart from being easily accessed by all involved in the project, Google Docs runs no risk of losing material; everything that is added to or taken away from a document is automatically saved, unlike Microsoft Office and similar software. With that said, Google Docs is also very easily reformatted for Microsoft Office, PDF files, etc. for the purposes of presentations or sharing the documents with others who may prefer a different software.

Once these forums are established and the preliminary research is underway, the next step is to compose a thesis. A thesis is a statement or theory that is put forward to be maintained and/or proved by way of scholarly research and persuasive writing. In its most basic form, a thesis is an opinion or an idea that is supported by credible sources. When creating a thesis, it is important to consult the prompt or the main idea of the project at hand. From there, one must form an opinion regarding the main idea and find credible sources with which to support that opinion.

After the thesis is formed, the next part of the process is to compile sources and quotes. Using the initial Pinterest board as well as any additional sources, one must go through the sources that have been selected and verify their credibility. If it is a website that is in question, a good indication of a website's authenticity is whether the domain is .org, .gov, or .edu. These domain names indicate that the information has not been changed by users or readers and has been verified by a reliable source. However, this is never a guarantee. The most credible sources are gathered through library databases and online resources such as JSTOR, Project Muse, and similar scholarly search engines. By closely reading these sources, one is able to pull out and cite quotes and passages that can or may be of use in support of the thesis. When the useful sources have been identified and analyzed, it is important to maintain a working bibliography or works cited page that can be added to or updated in the future. This can be very easily done on websites such as BibMe.com and EasyBib.com, which provide automatic citation in a variety of formats: MLA, APA, Chicago, etc.

By revisiting the thesis with the new research information, it is now possible to create and connect the various topics and ideas of the project. It is helpful to create sections for the project and treat each section like a smaller project. This way, those collaborating on the project can clearly tell the different sections apart and find creative ways to connect each section back to the original thesis. When connecting the sections of a large project, it is vital to constantly refer back to the thesis and ensure the project has as much continuity as possible.

In order to effectively consolidate the final project, the most important steps are to proofread and check the format so that the project is cohesive, clear, and consistent. It is also necessary to go back to the bibliography or works cited page and make sure that this information is still accurate and that the format is consistent with the rest of the project. Once properly formatted and edited, it is absolutely necessary to go over all of the material with every collaborator and apply constructive criticism; this part of the process guarantees that everyone involved is on the same page and that all participants are pleased with the work.

This process may not seem very different from a traditional research process; however, this process is unique in that it focuses on the importance of integrating modern technology into classic research techniques. The goal of this process is to encourage collaboration and to show the validity of integrating a new look at research into the professional standards. As an early career individual, I feel very strongly that the goal behind this research process has been achieved through my collaboration with Professor Jaen. We were able to work together using his years of knowledge and experience with my writing skills and modern technological approach to research. Through this process, we both learned a great deal and were able to grow both as a mentor and a mentee.

I am eternally grateful for the opportunities that have been awarded to me by Professor Jaen, the USITT Costume Commission, and the University of Massachusetts Boston Undergraduate Research Funding.

Colleen Fitzgibbons graduated summa cum laude from the University of Massachusetts Boston in May 2016, achieving a Bachelor's Degree in English and a minor in Theatre Arts. She was nominated and vetted for the 2015 Student Leadership Initiative at USITT among MFA students; she presented the research techniques utilized in her work on the Joseph P. Healy Grant awarded to Rafael Jaen in 2014. Colleen is collaborating on a journal article that examines the use of a historical figure as a vehicle for teaching and preserving the art of haute couture while reinforcing modern teaching techniques.

Talking to the Director

During the first conversations with a director, I discuss my impressions about the characters' core emotions, qualities, and actions. The goal is to integrate her/his ideas with mine. Once I have a sense of the character's spine (internal world), I can come up with a point of view to help me access their motivations and secrets. This deep investigation helps me choose just the right costume element to bring each character to life. For example, I can give a shawl to an actress in a period drama, and suggest that she loosens it during a seduction scene. I can also give an actor a wallet full of (fake) dollar bills to carry in his pocket as a visual clue or reminder of their character's status.

Other important things to chat about during the first meetings include the needs stated in the script. I make sure to include them as I begin to build each character's closet. I also look for iconic costume items that will endow each character with meaning, foreshadowing their journey through the play. I call this the "character's armor." In *Edith Can Shoot Things and Hit Them*, one example of Edith's "armor" would be a pair of short, distressed, blue overalls; they give her the ability to roam freely and hang from the barn's rafters. There is also her red shirt, which represents the feral side of her personality, as well as her love for her brother and her passion for what's right.

The Aristotelian Model

Another useful tool, in preparing items for discussion, is the Aristotelian model. I look at the three so-called unities of time, place, and action for each scene. These are important because they will help define what folks are wearing from scene to scene. For example, a character could be dressed casually during the daytime, while seated by a fireplace at home. Later in the action she/he may be going out in the middle of a bitter winter night. This would warrant a change or an addition of costume. Sometimes these aspects are clearly defined in the script, and other times, there is room for changes, attributions, and personal interpretation by the designer. In addition, I identify the cathartic moment(s) that can inform a character's journey. This can help me create a costume arc depicting (or supporting) the character's evolution from the beginning, to the middle, and end of the play. For example, when looking at the characters Stanley and Blanche Dubois in Tennessee William's *A Streetcar Named Desire*, I could use their character's analysis to choose the proper sequencing of costumes and foreshadow what comes next (in each scene) for them. In her essay *Blanche Dubois: An Antihero*, Lauren Siegle writes a compelling thesis that could be used as a design concept. She states:

Williams's vilification of Stanley throughout the entire play draws a clear distinction between victim and villain in the rape scene. Upon Stanley's first appearance, Williams describes how '[h]e seizes women up at a glance . . . crude images flashing into his mind and determining the way he smiles at them,' and in the next line Blanche not coincidentally 'draw[s] involuntarily back from his stare' (25). This significant exchange sets the mood for the tension between Blanche and Stanley that continues throughout the play. Several times Blanche regards Stanley with a 'look of panic' (127) or a 'frightened look' (135).

Later, Siegle adds:

In addition to the iconic comment 'I have always depended on the kindness of strangers' (178), Blanche's vulnerability is also illuminated

through stage directions such as 'a look of sorrowful perplexity as though all human experience shows on her face' (167) and 'She turns her face to [the doctor] and stares at him with desperate pleading' (177–8).

I could look at this relationship as a cat and mouse game. Stanley would be the lecherous man, and women in general would be his prey. I could use the image of a stray tomcat as a metaphor for him and a white mouse for Blanche. I could also add dark-red (blood) fabric to Stanley's costume for the rape scene, foreshadowing the violent act he will carry out. At the end, her brightness gone, Blanche could wear gray (dead mouse) shades. Though this explanation is an oversimplification of the process, it illustrates how visual language can help create a character arc that tells and supports the story.[6]

Historical Context: Using Human Geography as a Framework

I like researching the history of fashion pertinent to the characters of a play, to learn about the particulars of a time period. This gives me a sense of how people lived (or are living) during specific times. Human geography is the perfect framework for this, for it is "the study of the many cultural aspects found throughout the world and how they relate to the spaces and places where they originate and then travel as people continually move across various areas." This science looks at varied phenomena such as language, religion, socio-economic structures, art, music, and other aspects that "explain how and/or why people function as they do in the areas in which they live."[7]

For example, when analyzing an Elizabethan play, it will be important to differentiate social rank and class that existed among Queen Elizabeth's subjects. During the late 1500s, the Queen passed a series of strict dress code laws. These regulations allowed her to curb extravagant spending on imported goods. While the royals and other upper classes wore regulated clothes with unique silhouettes, rich fabrics, and fancy trimmings (keeping them at the top of the class pole), the common folks were still wearing basic garments dating to medieval times. There were also colors and embroideries specific to social stature. Those found dressed in inappropriate clothing could be fined. The British Library (online) includes the original transcript about these laws in the document *Elizabeth I's Proclamation Against Excess*.[8]

For the play *Edith Can Shoot Things and Hit Them*, I looked at the 1990s for fashion and cultural references. The script tells us about the type of music, TV, and comic books that were part of the pop culture. The playwright A. Rey Pamatmat also describes the play's location as a "remote non-working farm outside of a remote town in remotest Middle America." This was relevant because it helped me determine what is in the kids' closets. My assumption was that Edith and Kenny got their everyday clothes at a small town general store (a store with small offerings of a variety of goods). I reached this logical conclusion because they fended for themselves, and because this is before online shopping was the norm. In Benji's case, his mother buys his clothes—most probably by mail order from an L. L. Bean catalog. The action takes place before the Internet after all! All these facts are of importance when talking to a director, and they can be helpful later when making scene-specific costume choices.

The "W" Questions or the "Nuts and Bolts"

I like to approach the "nuts and bolts" of each act or scene by using "W" questions; these include What, Why, Who, When, and Where. For example:

1. **W**hat is the play, act, or scene about? This would refer to the main themes and subthemes in the story.

2. **W**hy is it meaningful? This refers to the reasons why the show will be produced, and why it is important to the company and audience.

3. **W**ho are the characters, including protagonist, antagonist, etc.? This can be used when choosing character color palettes. For example, the protagonist (or main character in a drama) and the antagonist (or chief opponent) could wear complementary colors that would put them at opposite ends of the color wheel, supporting the idea that the characters are adversaries in the play.

4. **W**hen is the story taking place? This could refer to the time of day, as well as the time of year. In some eras, day wear was very different from evening wear. Also, seasonal clothing will vary greatly the further away the play's location is from the Equator.

5. **W**here is the story taking place? This is specific to the location. Is it indoors or outdoors? Is it in a specific country? Is it in the countryside or a coastal town?

The final objective, regardless of what method you choose to use, is to do a thorough script and character analysis that can allow you to design costumes that are a living and breathing part of the storytelling. They can't be precious untouchable things; they have to be accessible to the audience and useful to the actors. They also have to help tell the story.

Stage Directions: The Spoken Word and the Playwright's Notes

What are stage directions? They are instructions in the text of a play, indicating blocking, tone of an action, sound effects, lighting, etc. They are usually within brackets, and mixed in with dialogue. They are directed to the actors and the stage crew, and they are not spoken. They are important points of reference; they could indicate the playwright's wishes, or the notations from a very first production. Let's look at the following example:

Six Characters in Search of an Author
(*Sei personaggi in cerca d'autore*)

A COMEDY IN THE MAKING

By Luigi Pirandello

[1921]

English version by

Edward Storer

[New York: E. P. Dutton, 1922]

ACT I

Daytime. The Stage of a Theatre

N.B. The Comedy is without acts or scenes. The performance is interrupted once, without the curtain being lowered, when the manager and the chief characters withdraw to arrange the scenario. A second interruption of the action takes place when, by mistake, the stage hands let the curtain down.

The spectators will find the curtain raised and the stage as it usually is during the daytime. It will be half dark, and empty, so that from the beginning the public may have the impression of an impromptu performance. Prompter's box and a small table and chair for the manager.

Two other small tables and several chairs scattered about as during rehearsals.

The ACTORS *and* ACTRESSES *of the company enter from the back of the stage: first one, then another, then two together; nine or ten in all. They are about to rehearse a Pirandello play:* Mixing It Up. [Il giuoco delle parti.] *Some* of the company move off towards their dressing rooms. The PROMPTER *who has the "book" under his arm, is waiting for the manager in order to begin the rehearsal.*

The ACTORS *and* ACTRESSES, *some standing, some sitting, chat and smoke. One perhaps reads a paper; another cons his part.*

Finally, the MANAGER *enters and goes to the table prepared for him. His* SECRETARY *brings him his mail, through which he glances. The* PROMPTER *takes his seat, turns on a light, and opens the "book."*

The Manager [*throwing a letter down on the table*]. I can't see. [*To* PROPERTY MAN.] Let's have a little light, please!

Property Man. Yes, sir, yes, at once. [*A light comes down on to the stage.*]

The Manager [*clapping his hands*]. Come along! Come along! Second act of "Mixing It Up." [*Sits down.*] [*The* ACTORS *and* ACTRESSES *go from the front of the stage to the wings, all except the three who are to begin the rehearsal.*]

The Prompter [*reading the "book"*]. "Leo Gala's house. A curious room serving as dining-room and study."

The Manager [*to* PROPERTY MAN]. Fix up the old red room.

Property Man [*noting it down*]. Red set. All right!

The Prompter [*continuing to read from the "book"*]. "Table already laid and writing desk with books and papers. Bookshelves. Exit rear to Leo's bedroom. Exit left to kitchen. Principal exit to right."

The Manager [*energetically*]. Well, you understand: The principal exit over there; here, the kitchen. [*Turning to actor who is to play the part of* SOCRATES.] You make your entrances and exits here. [*To* PROPERTY MAN.] The baize doors at the rear, and curtains.

Property Man [*noting it down*]. Right!

The Prompter [*reading as before*]. "When the curtain rises, Leo Gala, dressed in cook's cap and apron, is busy beating an egg in a cup. Philip, also dressed as a cook, is beating another egg. Guido Venanzi is seated and listening."

Leading Man [*To* MANAGER]. Excuse me, but must I absolutely wear a cook's cap?

The Manager [*annoyed*]. I imagine so. It says so there anyway. [*Pointing to the "book."*]

Leading Man. But it's ridiculous![9]

This opening scene of *Six Characters in Search of an Author* shows the (Production) Manager using the script's stage direction to justify his work, and to stop the main actor's complaints. Most of the directors with whom I have collaborated start by analyzing scripts and doing dramaturgical research. While they look for ways to implement the ideas of the playwright, they also discuss the things that may hinder the audience experience and take away from clear storytelling.

Stage directions are especially helpful to me as a designer, when they indicate the mood and general environment of a scene. Nevertheless, a director and design team may decide to reinterpret them in the final product. This particular approach may attract criticism from audiences and theatre connoisseurs, as it continues to provoke debate among scholars and critics alike. For example, in an article from 2003 Jean Schiffman wrote:

Many of us were taught to cross out stage directions on the first reading. In *A Challenge to the Actor*, Uta Hagen advises ignoring 'all adjectives and descriptive adverbs' written into the script; they are meant for the readers, not the actors. Actors should concern themselves with what they do—their actions—not with predetermining how they do it. She reminds us that Shakespeare used few stage directions.[10]

Most recently, *The Guardian* posted a comprehensive article by Chris Wilkinson.[11] In it he wrote:

It is often said that we have a culture which is slavishly subservient to the text – that the job is to serve the writer's vision and not impose anything on top of this. . . . There is, however, one notable area where writers' intentions are frequently ignored – their stage directions. Whilst dialogue is sacrosanct, all the playwright's other notes about a character's actions, emotional state or the setting of a scene are often seen as at best optional, and at worst, things to be actively ignored. There are a number of reasons for this. It is partly historical – after all it is widely assumed that most stage directions in Shakespeare are not the author's own (though some may have been added by colleagues) and therefore not authentic. And sometimes, as in most Samuel French playtexts, the stage directions in a script are little more than a record of how the play was originally staged. Yet for many actors and directors, there is a more fundamental reason for ignoring these authorial notes – they are seen as an attempt by the writer to muscle in and do their job for them. . . . This is an understandable view. But I often find, when reading plays, that a good writer can not only communicate an enormous amount in that italicized text between the characters' speech, but that, in some circumstances, the more demanding the stage directions, then the more creative freedom that the director has.

The Importance of a Good Dramaturge

In my experience, dramaturges are friendly in-house production critics. They research, analyze text, and seek expert answers to production questions. They are an extraordinary resource for the director, playwright, actors, and designers. The Literary Managers and Dramaturges of the Americas (LMDA) website defines the role as follows:

Over the past three decades, the role of the dramaturge and literary manager has expanded in the United States and Canada alongside the increasing importance of contemporary playwriting. Working in theatres and playwrights' organizations, in colleges and universities, and on a project-by-project basis, dramaturges contextualize the world of a play; establish connections among the text, actors, and audience; offer opportunities for playwrights; generate projects and programs; and create conversations about plays in their communities. In the ecology of theatre-making, dramaturges and literary managers forge a critical link between artists and institutions, and institutions and their communities. They work with their other artistic collaborators to hone their vision, focus their goals and find outlets for their creative work on new and classical plays and dance pieces. Dramaturges and literary managers serve the field as experts on our dramatic past and as advocates for writers of today and the important work of the future. Literary Managers and Dramaturges of the Americas (LMDA) connects dramaturges and literary managers together with their director, writer, actor, academic and student colleagues in ways that impact the culture and landscape of theatre in North America and, more recently, abroad.[12]

For the show *Edith Can Shoot Things and Hit Them*, dramaturge Alexandra Juckno wrote many relevant topics. They ranged from Filipino food, to family relations, and the Midwest landscape. All of these disparate essays responded to specific elements of the script and ended up helping the production team. It helped us when making choices that supported the sensibility of the story. In my case, she even helped me to make choices about the season, and the passing of days, based on subtleties in the language. One excellent sample, which supported my theory about Kenny and Edith being parentified children, is represented in the following entry.

"Even though EDITH shows the kids dealing positively with their loss, Dad's grief-stricken situation is one not uncommon among Asian-Americans, especially those who have emigrated to America." She goes on to indicate that poet Julie Feng has written about how "Asian-American communities are affected by mental health illnesses such as depression and the attendant stigmas attached to admitting to suffering. Julie [Feng] links to studies that highlight connections between mental health disorders and factors like immigration, acculturation, assimilation, and inter-generational trauma." . . . "One interesting connection between these factors and the play is the way Rey [Pamatmat] plays with the characters' isolation—Edith and Kenny, though geographically isolated, retain a strong connection to Mother and to their house, land, and Benji; Dad's isolation keeps growing as he runs from his mistakes and is self-imposed. Feng aligns with Kenny and Edith, advocating connection and communication as ways to combat the stigmatization of mental illness and grief. She says, 'Parents, guardians, spouses, siblings, friends, teachers, doctors, and counselors need to be vigilant. They need to believe the people in their lives. This is a problem than can be fixed – as long as we actively decide to do better.' Throughout EDITH, we see the kids strive against all odds to stay together and stay bonded—from Kenny and Benji surreptitiously passing notes in class to Edith breaking out of school to reunite with her brother."[13]

Given that dramaturges have to answer to so many masters, to me they are also the ultimate diplomats.

Talking with the Actors

I like to establish a relationship with the actors from the get-go. I collect key information early on and I compile it in my Web folders. Since most of my work in regional theatre is in Equity Houses, sometimes the actors are hired weeks in advance, and before the rehearsal period starts. In this case, I will contact them via email, and ask for their basic measurements, special needs or concerns, hairstyles, and current headshots. This information will come in handy during the costume rendering process.

I also like to attend first readings (whenever possible) and full company meetings in order to ascertain what the actors are like. This will help me decide the best approach in supporting them. Like in any collaboration or situation, some will be trusting from the very beginning while others may seem suspicious. If an actor comes across as being "needy," I listen to them carefully and take notice of what may be worrisome. For example, I had a situation where an actress seemed to obsess a bit too much about the heels that she was expected to wear. This was for a play set in Victorian times, and she was adamant about the style of shoes that she wanted, which were modern looking. After paying attention to her walk, I asked if she had had foot-surgery recently. Bingo! She'd had a bunion (swelling on the first joint of the big toe) removed, and she had just started to walk without a cast, but she wasn't completely healed yet. I talked to the producers, and we provided different shoe options for rehearsals, and by the first week of performance, she could wear real leather, low heel, Victorian boots. We also had them stretched and padded.

Paying attention, quietly observing, and then talking in private with the actress allowed me to come up with a design solution that supported all involved. Costume designers must always be vigilant.

Obtaining Basic Information

When I first contact the actors via email, I ask them for a JPEG of a current headshot. I even prefer an iPhone selfie rather than a ten-year-old photo, and sometimes I even Google the actors and look for pictures from recent productions. I also ask for a current measurement sheet. If they do not have one, I email them an "Actor's Commercial Size Survey" (see box ahead). This questionnaire contains 16 questions that help me get a sense of their body shape, existing fabric allergies, and the presence of visible tattoos. I don't want to see the actor break into hives (if they are allergic to wool, for example) or display a tattoo that does not go with their character.

Actor's Commercial Size Survey

1. Please email me a current headshot.

2. What is your height?

3. What is your weight?

4. What is your commercial blouse/dress shirt size? (Note: Since commercial sizes vary, please name specific brands.)

5. What is your commercial pant size with inseam? (Note: Since commercial sizes vary, please name specific brands.)

6. What is your commercial dress/suit size? (Note: Since commercial sizes vary, please name specific brands.)

7. What is your bra size?

8. What is your t-shirt size?

9. What is your tights and/or shorts size?

10. What is your waist size?

11. What is your hair color and length?

12. What is your shoe size and special needs (wide, extra-wide, no heel, etc.)?

13. Do you have fabric and/or detergent allergies?

14. Do you have visible tattoos; where? And do you own tattoo-covering makeup?

15. Do you have visible piercings, including ears, nose, etc.?

16. Are there other notes?

Often, actors are aware of their commercial sizes, but in some instances, they are not. I keep information on file, in my digital archives, to use as a reference when trying to ascertain if an individual is giving me accurate facts. Sometimes, different actors may be very close in sizing, so I can compare them and then pull, drape, or buy specific costume pieces ahead of time. In other instances, when working with new performers especially, I pay careful attention to discrepancies. For example, if a (new) actor "A" writes that he is 5'8" tall, weighs 200 lbs, and wears a suit size 42R, I can check my existing files for actor "B," whom I have worked with before, and who wears a size 42R. He is 5'11", weighs 170 lbs, and has a 32" waist. This data tells me that actor "A"'s information is inaccurate or out of date, and it would be safe to assume that he is probably a size 50R, with a 46" waist; similar to actor "C," whose information I also have on file. In a situation like the one described, I will pull costumes based on my data rather than what the actor emailed me.

After years of experience, I can usually discern when the information that I receive is off the mark. Costume designers must remember that mistakes like this are likely to happen and they need to correct them ahead of time. It is important to embrace all body types and to make sure that the actors feel at ease during costume fittings.

Establishing the Character's "Spine": Underlying Motivations, Back-Story, Secrets, etc.

Once I start research and preliminary sketches, I send the actors a second email with links to my research on Pinterest, or Google Slides (see Figure 1.6), and I also ask if they have some early ideas about their character. I always do this with the director's permission. I often anticipate that the actors are ready to start a conversation because in Equity Houses, the actors are expected to be off-book by the second week of rehearsal—depending on the schedule. Most experienced folks are happy to chat early rather than wait till the first fitting. I ask the following two questions:

1. What are the character's underlying motivations, back-story, secrets, etc.?

2. What are the character's core emotions, qualities, and actions?

I can use the information to foreshadow a character's journey; from dark to light, from overwhelmed to clear, or from immature to grown-up. I can also "translate" emotions, qualities, and actions into textures and colors to add visual meaning to the story.

Establishing Digital Collaboration with the Actors Prior to Fittings

In preparation for fittings, I email the actors links to the final sketches. In some cases, these are slides of research boards with visual information (Figure 1.6). For *Edith Can Shoot Things and Hit Them*, I emailed them a link to a complete set of research boards scene-by-scene with notes. This worked as a visual costume breakdown and helped facilitate the 54

Edith Can Shoot Things

Company One June 2015
Director; Shawn LaCount
Costumes: Rafael Jaen

Edith – But to execute this mission — our mission — you have to stand up and face things and say: "Hey! Who goes there?"

Maria Jan Carreon

Faded color tints and grays for Edith. Ends with more girl like colors such as lavender some Benji's plaid?

FIGURE 1.6

Sample of a preliminary research sheet for a character. I used Google Slides for this, and emailed the link to the actors. The image includes basic information about color, style, and silhouette. It is a visual representation of what's in the character's closet. The images include potential shopping items, color palette, and the headshot of actress Maria Jan Carreon.

quick-changes that took place in the show (see Figures 1.7–1.10). My final objective is to create a (digital) collaborative environment, before I start working with the actors in the fitting room and during the rehearsal process.

FIGURE 1.7

I compiled 25 slides for *Edith Can Shoot Things and Hit Them*. These two samples represent the scenes "Changing" and "Space is Infinite."

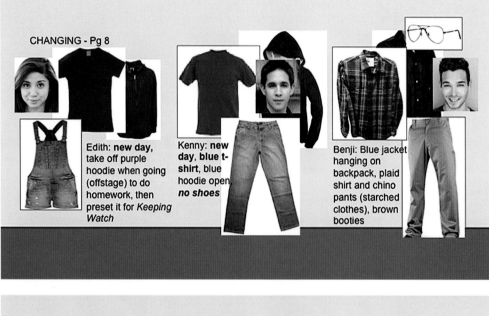

CHANGING - Pg 8

Edith: **new day,** take off purple hoodie when going (offstage) to do homework, then preset it for *Keeping Watch*

Kenny: **new day, blue t-shirt,** blue hoodie open, **no shoes**

Benji: Blue jacket hanging on backpack, plaid shirt and chino pants (starched clothes), brown booties

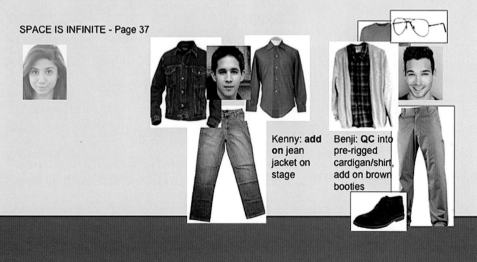

SPACE IS INFINITE - Page 37

Kenny: **add on** jean jacket on stage

Benji: **QC** into pre-rigged cardigan/shirt, add on brown booties

FIGURE 1.8

The slides include Web images, and some actual photos of the garments that I used. The actor's headshots are included from left to right: Maria Jan Carreon, Gideon Bautista, and Eddie Shields. A great thing about Google Slides is that I could make notations and update the information on the spot during rehearsals, and I could also add or delete images as needed.

FIGURE 1.9

These photos from *Edith Can Shoot Things and Hit Them* are the corresponding images from the production; they are from the scenes "Changing" and "Space is Infinite."

FIGURE 1.10

For Edith (Maria Jan Carreon), I introduce the purple color to signify change or transmutation, and for Benji (Eddie Shields), I am using muted secondary colors to have him blend with the set—signaling that he belongs in this home, and foreshadowing events to come. The theatre was small and intimate, so I could get away with this choice without losing the actor on the stage!

Testimonial

SHAWN LACOUNT—ARTISTIC DIRECTOR AND DIRECTOR

When directors champion concept, it limits the potential for complex design choices because it is easier for designers to design to a concept rather than to design for the play holistically.

Bio

Shawn LaCount is the co-founder of Company One Theatre. Recent directorial credits include the regional premieres of Jackie Sibblies Drury's *Really*; Young Jean Lee's *We're Gonna Die* (the American Repertory Theatre/Company One Theatre); A. Rey Pamatmat's *Edith Can Shoot Things and Hit Them* (Elliot Norton Award Nominee for Outstanding Director and Outstanding Production); Annie Baker's *The Flick* (Elliot Norton Award, Outstanding Production); the world premiere of Kirsten Greenidge's *Splendor* (IRNE Award nominee, Best New Play); the Boston premieres of *Bengal Tiger at the Baghdad Zoo* by Rajiv Joseph; *The Elaborate Entrance of Chad Deity* by Kristoffer Diaz (Elliot Norton Award for Outstanding Director and Outstanding Production); Annie Baker's *The Aliens* (Elliot Norton Award for Outstanding Director and Outstanding Production); the world premiere of *Grimm* (IRNE Award nominee for Best New Play); the Boston premiere of *The Overwhelming* by J. T. Rogers (Elliot Norton Award Nominee, Outstanding Production); the Boston premiere of Haruki Murakami's *After the Quake* (Elliot Norton Award Nominee, Outstanding Production); Stephen Sondheim's ASSASSINS (IRNE nomination for Best Director and Best Musical); and the Boston premiere of Noah Haidle's *Mr. Marmalade* (Elliot Norton Award Nominee, Outstanding Director/Outstanding Drama). Shawn holds an MA Ed. in Theatre Education from Clark University and an MFA in Directing from the University of Massachusetts, Amherst. He has taught at Emerson College, Boston Arts Academy, Huntington Theatre Company, Tufts University, Stage One, and the University of Massachusetts, Amherst.

Interview

Rafael: What are your beliefs (or approach) in regard to collaborating with designers?

Shawn: Listen. When working with designers, it is essential that I hear all of their immediate thoughts before I express my own. I operate the same way with actors. This way, I have honest context for where my co-artists are coming from, where they are meeting the text before I even begin expressing my own views. Sometimes I fully agree with my collaborators' initial ideas and vision, but more often than not, we have different points of entry on any given play. Embracing the multiplicity of voices and ideas is what makes for great theatre. It also requires designers and actors and all parties involved to take ownership and pride in the work they are part of creating. As a director, I believe that my job is to hear and acknowledge, curate, refine, and merge these thoughts and ideas into one piece of art that is necessarily better than it would have been if only one or two people were visioning and creating it.

Rafael: Is there a "mantra" or core belief that you subscribe to when directing a production?

Shawn: Get out of the way. I generally think that directors get in the way of the play (and their collaborators) when they feel compelled to infuse some specific vision or concept on top of a play. When directors champion a concept, it limits the potential for complex design choices because it is easier for designers to design to a concept rather than to design for the play holistically. Too often a director's concept simplifies a play that might be beautifully complicated by design. This results in a few spectacular moments in an otherwise flat audience experience of mediocre theatre. I feel directors need to be responsible to the play before their own theory. The danger here is about ego. When this approach is most successful, the director disappears and the performers and the playwright are the stars. In my humble opinion, this is how it should be.

Rafael: In your experience, what makes for an effective theatre collaboration?

Shawn: It is important that the designers know how necessary they are to the process and that if they trust the play and our process together, that we will likely make one of the most authentic, memorable, and moving pieces of theatre in any given season.

Design Gallery: *Edith Can Shoot Things and Hit Them*

Company One. Summer 2015. "*Edith Can Shoot Things and Hit Them.*" Playwright and Production Staff. Playwright: A. Rey Pamatmat, Director: Shawn LaCount, Dramaturgy: Alexandra Juckno, Scenic Designer: Cristina M. Todesco, Costume Designer: Rafael Jaen, Sound Designer: Ed Young, Lighting Designer: Jen Rock, Props Master: Molly Fitz Maurice, Stage Manager: Kevin Deane Parker.

INTERMISSION

Edith: change into white uniform shirt (under-dress), purple hoodie, and black shorts. Preset red jacket.

Kenny: change into gray thermal shirt, jeans and green plaid jacket

Benji: change into orange t-shirt, brown plaid pajama pants and Kenny's jean jacket

FIGURE 1.11

These are two more samples of the show *Edith Can Shoot Things and Hit Them* from the 25 slides in my Google folder.

FIGURE 1.12

I added an extra slide with costume notations during the "Intermission"—for the wardrobe crew and the actors. For "Homecoming" (the last scene), I added prints that symbolize the changes in the characters. Edith finds her music, Kenny's horizons have widened, and Benji is in greener pastures. The slides include Web images, and some actual photos of the garments that I used. The actor's headshots are included from left to right: Maria Jan Carreon, Gideon Bautista, and Eddie Shields.

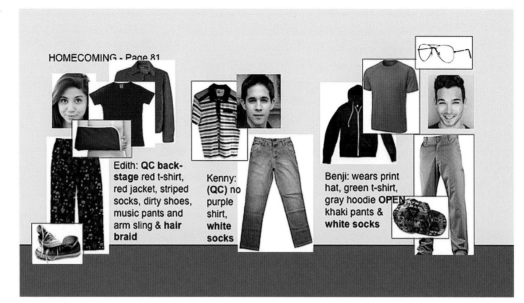

HOMECOMING - Page 81

Edith: QC back-stage red t-shirt, red jacket, striped socks, dirty shoes, music pants and arm sling & **hair braid**

Kenny: (QC) no purple shirt, **white socks**

Benji: wears print hat, green t-shirt, gray hoodie **OPEN** khaki pants & **white socks**

FIGURE 1.13 and FIGURE 1.14

These photos are from the scenes "Space is Infinite" and "Homecoming." In the first image (Figure 1.13), Benji (Eddie Shields) and Kenny (Gideon Bautista) are on a date. I am using some complementary color details (orange and blue) to show that they are at opposite ends at that point of the story. The second photo (Figure 1.14) is from the last scene; notice the vivid colors and prints of the costumes and the props.

FIGURE 1.14

Citations and Sources

1   Shawn LaCount, co-founder of Company One
     Theatre, Boston, MA. Accessed July 05, 2015. https://
     companyone.org/about-us/staff-board/

2   "Edith Can Shoot Things and Hit Them." Accessed
     July 5, 2015. http://companyone.org/production/
     edith-can-shoot-things-and-hit-them/

3   Allan Schwartz, LCSW, PhD. "Family Boundaries and
     the Parentified Child," Dr. Schwartz' Weblog. Written
     on March 13, 2012. Accessed July 2, 2015. www.
     mentalhelp.net/blogs/family-boundaries-and-the-
     parentified-child/

4   "Overview Google Docs, Sheets, and Slides."
     Accessed July 2, 2015. https://support.google.com/
     docs/answer/49008?hl=en

5   "Joseph P. Healey Research Grant Program."
     Internal Funding Programs, Joseph P. Healey
     Research Grant Program – University of
     Massachusetts Boston. Accessed July 28,
     2016. www.umb.edu/research/info_for_faculty_
     staff/research_funding_sources/internal_
     funding_programs/healey_research_grant_
     program

6   Lauren Siegle, *Blanche Dubois: BU Arts and Science
     Program Web Journal*. Accessed July 21, 2015.

www.bu.edu/writingprogram/journal/past-issues/
issue-2/seigle/. Williams, Tennessee, *A Streetcar
Named Desire*. New York: New Directions Publishing
Corporation, 2004. Print.

7   Amanda Briney. "Human Geography—An Overview."
About.com. Accessed June 9, 2015. http://
geography.about.com/od/culturalgeography/a/
humangeography.htm

8   Elizabeth I's "Proclamation Against Excess,"
1577. Accessed June 9, 2015. www.bl.uk/learning/
timeline/item126628.html

9   Luigi Pirandello. "Six Characters in Search of an
Author." [1921]. English version by Edward Storer.

[New York: E. P. Dutton, 1922]. Accessed June 20,
2015. www.eldritchpress.org/lp/six.htm.

10 Schiffman, Jean. "Taking Directions." Backstage.
com. March 3, 2003. Accessed November 28, 2015.
www.backstage.com/news/taking-directions.

11 "Chris Wilkinson." *The Guardian*. Accessed July 24,
2016. www.theguardian.com/profile/chriswilkinson

12 "The Role of the Dramaturge." Accessed July 22,
2015. www.lmda.org/dramaturgy.

13 Alexandra Juckno. "Memento Mori." May 27, 2015.
Accessed July 22, 2015. https://edithcanshootc1.
wordpress.com/2015/05/27/memento-mori/.

MY PRIMARY JOB IS TO SERVE THE PLAYWRIGHT

BY TELLING HIS/HER STORY.

SPIRO VELOUDOS, DIRECTOR[1]

CHAPTER TWO

THE DIGITAL COSTUME BIBLE & DESIGN STUDIO

I have grown fond of creating digital costume project folders in a shared Internet file. I compile information in Dropbox, Google Docs, Pinterest, etc. for access on the go; they all have apps that are easy to install on iPhone and Android phones. In this chapter, we'll look at some useful nuts and bolts, and I will use as a sample my design work for *Kiss Me Kate* produced by the Lyric Stage Company of Boston.

The Digital Costume Bible

Before telling a character's story in a costume sketch, there are preparatory steps. One of the most valuable tools that I learned during my school years at NYU included the importance of creating a Costume Bible.

A costume Bible is an invaluable book created by the costume designer for a show, movie, etc. In more professional theatres, the assistant designer makes and updates the Bible. It is a compilation of ALL paperwork and information needed to costume that particular show or event.[2]

It includes a monthly and weekly calendar with deadlines, costume plot, and breakdowns; budget and labor spreadsheets; copy of sketches and fabric samples; fashion and shopping/pulling research; actors' headshots and compiled measurements; director and rehearsal notes, etc.

The Digital Costume Plot

The costume plot is a chart that tracks the characters and their costume changes throughout a show. I use Microsoft Excel or Google Sheets to create it, organizing it with rows and columns. The act/scene information goes in the top rows, and the character's information goes in the left columns.

After dividing the play script into acts and scenes, I type the information into the top row cells, going left to right. For example, I will start with Act I/Scene 1,

continuing with Act I/Scene 2, and so on. I then type each actor's name and their character in the left columns, in alphabetical order, and one per row. For reference, I include their character's characteristics, such as status, age, etc. These notes can be really helpful when working in a large cast show or when actors play multiple roles to keep track of who plays who in each scene.

I track costumes in the intercepting Act/Scenes rows and Actor/Character columns. For example, if character A is listed in row 4 and shows up in the Act I/Scene 5 column, I will enter an "X" in the intersecting cell denoting that we see the actor on stage (and in costume) then and there.

I also like to add brief descriptions of each scene including location, season, time of the day, etc. This information will help me later, when I start planning costume changes, while reading the costume plot. Looking at the previous example, if Act I/Scene 5 says that it is winter and it is snowing, I could add a note next to character A's X saying that her/his coat, hat, and gloves will come off when entering the room in that scene.

Finally, it's also important to track each character's costume changes by adding a number next to their X in a row (e.g., X1, X2, X3, etc.) each time the actor changes as the play or musical progresses. This tracking helps us know when the character changes or when they stay in the same costume from scene to scene. In the previous example, if we see character A for the first time in Act I/Scene 5, I would write X1. If the character was wearing the same costume in Act I/Scene 6 I would enter X1 again, but if they changed clothes I would enter X2.

The last column of the costume plot shows a tally of the number of costumes each actor will have based on the number of costume changes (X1, X2, X3) each character has in the script. This tracking system helps us to budget accurately.

Lyric Stage's "Kiss Me Kate" Costume Plot

	ACTOR AND/OR DANCER	CHARACTER (S)	ACT I SCENE 1	SCENE 2	Scene 3	SCENE 4	SCENE 5			SCENE 6	SCENE 7	SCENE 8	SCENE 9	INTERMISSION
			Notes: Ford's Theatre	Notes: Backstage	Notes: Dress Rooms	Notes: Padua	Notes: Market Square			Notes: Backstage	Notes: Dressing Room	Notes: Country Road	Notes: Church Square	
			Opening Act 1 -part 1 to 5	Why Can't you Behave	Wunderbar & So In Love	Padua: We Open in Venice	Tom, Dick and Harry	I have come to Wive it Wealthily in Padua	I Hate Men & Were Thine That Special Face	Lilli and Fred's Argument	1st and 2nd Man	Cantiamo D'Amore Wine	Finale Act I -Kiss Me Kate	
1	Arthur Waldstein	Pops -Doorman, Padua Priest, Half Donkey	X 1 X1	X1									X2 -Priest	
2	Mary Callahan*	Hattie - Lilli's Dresser AND Wardrobe Lady	X1 Hat off		X1								X2	
3	Kennedy Pugh*	Paul -Dresser, Ensemble Singer	X1 Jacket off	X1	X1								X2	
4	Phil Crumrine	Ralph Stage Manager, Singer, Half Donkey	X1		X1	X2-Donkey's Ass				X1		X2 Page Boy	X2	
5	Michele DeLuca	Lois Lane -Chanteuse, Bianca	X1-QC X2	X2 -AO	X3 Partial	X3 -Hat and Cape	X3 -Hat, cape off						X3	
6	Patrick Ryan	Bill Calhoun -hoofer, Lucencio	X1	X1 - Messy		X2 -Lucentio	X2						X2	
7	Amelia Broome*	Lilli Vanessi -Star, Katharine	X1-QC Hat, Jacket off		X2 QC X3	X3 -Hat and Cape			X3 -Hat, cape off	X3	X2		X4	
8	Peter Davenport*	Fred Graham - Producer/Director, Petruchio	X1		X2 QC X3	X3 - Petruchio - Hat and Cape		X3	X3	X3	X3		X3	
9	Jack Agneu	Harry Trevor -Veteran Actor, Baptista	X1 Jacket off			X2 -Baptista	X2	X2	X2				X2	
10	Santio Cupon	Male Ensemble, Harberdasher	X 1 QC X2 Dancer			X3 Harberdash	X3	X3				X3	X3	
11	Neil Casey*	1st Man -Gunman, Knight, Finale Donkey			X1 QC	X3 Donkey Head					X1		X2	
12	J.T.Turner*	2nd Man -Gunman, Knight, Finale Donkey			X1						X1		X2	
13	Peter Mills	Flynt -Dancer, Gremio -Suitor, Gen Aide	X1			X2 -leggings AO	X2 -Gremio	X2				X2	X2	
14	Joseph Cullinane*	Riley -Dancer, Philip P. Servant, Gen Aide, Hortensio -Suitor	X1			X2 -leggings AO	X2 - Hortensio	X2				X2	X2	
15	Josh Dennis	Ensemble, Cab Driver, Nathaniel servant, Howell's Driver	X 1 QC	X2 -Cab Driver		X3 Nathaniel	X3	X3				X3	X3	
16	Tim Smith*	Stage Hand, Inn Keeper, General Harrison Howell	X1 Stage Hand				X2 Inn Keeper						X2	
17	Caitlin Diana Doyle	Ensemble, Inn Waitress	X 1 QC Dress Off			X2A -QC Ring Girl	QC X3 - Waitress					X3	X3	
18	Caitlin Crosby Doonan*	Ensemble, Wench	X 1 QC Dress Off			X2A -QC Ring Girl			X3 Wench			X3 Wench	X3	
19	Hillary Werthman	Ensemble, Wench	X 1 QC Dress Off			X2A -QC Ring Girl			X3 Wench			X3 Wench	X3	
20	Rachel Bertone	Ensemble, Wench	X 1 QC Dress Off			X2A -QC Ring Girl			X3 Wench			X3 Wench	X3	
21	Shana Hevrly	Ensemble, Wench	X 1 QC Dress Off			X2A -QC Ring Girl			X3 Wench			X3 Wench	X3	

Prepared by Rafael Jaen 8/28/2009 Page 1

FIGURE 2.1

The Costume Plot (page 1) for the musical *Kiss Me Kate* at the Lyric Stage Company of Boston. With tracking, notes, and totals.

Lyric Stage's "Kiss Me Kate"   Costume Plot

#	ACTOR AND/OR DANCER	CHARACTER (S)	SCENE 1 — Notes: Theatre Alley		SCENE 2 — Notes: Shrew Show Curtain	SCENE 3 — Notes: Petruchio's House	SCENE 4 — Notes: Backstage Corridor	SCENE 5 — Notes: Dressing Room	SCENE 6 — Notes: Back Stage		SCENE 7 — Notes: Show Curtain	SCENE 8 — Notes: Garden of Baptista's House			TOTALS
			Entr'acte	Too Darn Hot - Song and Dance	Cancelled Mule Entrance	Where is the Life that I Lead	Always True to You in my Fashion	From this Moment On	Bianca & General's Enter	So In Love	Brush up you Shakespeare	Pavana	Women are so Simple	Finale Act II	
1	Arthur Waldstein	Pops -Doorman, Padua Priest, Half Donkey		X1-Partial			X1		X3-Partial			X3-Priest AO	X3 X3	X3	3
2	Mary Callahan*	Hattie - Lilli's Dresser AND Wardrobe Lady		X3 -No coat					X3 -with coat				X3	X3	3
3	Kennedy Pugh*	Paul -Dresser, Ensemble Singer		X1									X2	X2	2
4	Phil Crumrine	Ralph Stage Manager, Singer, Half Donkey		X1 Partial			X1						X3 AO	X3 AO	3
5	Michele DeLuca	Lois Lane -Chanteuse, Bianca					X4		X3-Partial			X3- AO	X3- AO	X3 AO	4
6	Patrick Ryan	Bill Calhoun -hoofer, Lucencio					X2- Partial		X2			X3	X3	X3	3
7	Amelia Broome*	Lilli Vanessi -Star, Katharine				X5 Ashes		X5 -Dior Hat QC	X6				X7	X7	6
8	Peter Davenport*	Fred Graham -Producer/Director, Petruchio			X4		X4	X4	X4	X4		X5	X5	X5	5
9	Jack Agneu	Harry Trevor -Veteran Actor, Baptista		X2 Partial								X3	X3	X3	3
10	Santio Cupon	Male Ensemble, Harberdasher		X3- Partial		X3 -Harberdasher QC	X1-Stage hand		X3			X4	X4	X4	4
11	Neil Casey*	1st Man -Gunman, Knight, Finale Donkey				X2	X2	X2		x2	X1- QC AO	X3- Donkey	X3- Donkey	X1- Reveal	3
12	J.T.Turner*	2nd Man -Gunman, Knight, Finale Donkey				X2	X2	X2		x2	X1- QC AO	X3- Donkey	X3- Donkey	X1- Reveal	3
13	Peter Mills	Flynt -Dancer, Gremio -Suitor		X2- Partial		X2 AO -Gregory QC	X3 -Gen Aide					X4	X4	X4	4
14	Joseph Cullinane*	Riley -Dancer, Philip P. Servant, Gen Aide, Hortensio -Suitor		X2- Partial		X2 AO -Philip QC	X3- Gen Aide					X4	X4	X5	5
15	Josh Dennis	Ensemble, Cab Driver, Nathaniel servant, Howell's Driver		X3- Partial		X3- Nathaniel QC	X4 Gen. Driver		X3 Partial QC X4			X5	X5	X5	5
16	Tim Smith*	Stage Hand, Inn Keeper, General Harrison Howell		X1 Partial			X3 Howell	X3	X3			X2 AO	X2	X2	3
17	Caitlin Diana Doyle	Ensemble, Inn Waitress		X4					X2- AO Crinoline			X5	X5	X5	5
18	Caitlin Crosby Doonan*	Ensemble, Wench		X4					X2- AO Crinoline			X5	X5	X5	5
19	Hillary Werthman	Ensemble, Wench		X4					X2- AO Crinoline			X5	X5	X5	5
20	Rachel Bertone	Ensemble, Wench		X4					X2- AO Crinoline			X5	X5	X5	5
21	Shana Hevrly	Ensemble, Wench		X4					X2- AO Crinoline			X5	X5	X5	5
													TOTALS	84

FIGURE 2.2

The Costume Plot (page 2). The quick-changes are highlighted to inform when costumes need to be quick-rigged (with snaps or velcro) for easy "in" or "out."

I like to include other notations such as AO (add-on), TO (take-off), QC (quick-change), etc. to indicate the addition of a garment on stage, taking off an item, etc. and plan if I need to quick-rig a closure with snaps, Velcro, etc. This information is very helpful to the wardrobe crew that will run the show.

It is important to mention that costume plots are a work in progress, and they will need updates throughout the process. After the first draft is complete, it is necessary to add new information based on rehearsal reports, director's notes, etc. continuously, until the last dress rehearsal. Having thorough information and tracking will help create accurate costume counts (see Figures 2.1 and 2.2).

The Digital Costume Piece List

The costume piece list form is an itemized breakdown chart that lists in detail what each character wears in each particular scene. It should match the information contained in the costume plot in regards to quick-changes, add-ons, etc. (see Figures 2.3 and 2.4). While there are some variations in the way designers do this task, I recommend making a costume piece list for each actor (including all the characters that they play) in spreadsheet form, and to give them copies to remind them what to wear.

I also create duplicate spreadsheets for the wardrobe crew containing more information; adding columns with the actor's measurements, laundry and dry-cleaning instructions, plus the costume sources. This approach helps the crew when replacing costume items (such as hosiery) during the run of the show, and with nightly inventories (to make sure that nothing is missing), laundry, and organizing (borrowed) costumes for returns after a show closes.

The Budget Specs: Including Builds, and Bought and Bought Items

It is important to create a preliminary budget spec to calculate expenses before hitting clothing and fabric stores. I include a budget and shopping receipt folder in my digital Costume Bible; it holds budget specs, receipts, rental agreements, etc. For budget specs and book-keeping, I recommend using an Excel (or Google Sheet) spreadsheet that includes pricing estimates of costume items by actor and sometimes by group, e.g., a dance shoe order for a specific musical number. Additionally, it is necessary to spec the cost of the builds or made to order (MTO) costumes, calculating the cost of labor, materials, and sewing supplies when pricing them.

As you shop, keep updating the budget specs to have an accurate tally of the remnant budget. If you hit a sale and save money in costume "a," you can use the savings for a necessary incidental in costume "b." Always make sure to save all Web order invoices and copies of in-person-shopping receipts in your digital folder. When I shop in person, I like taking pictures of receipts with my iPhone on the spot, uploading the images into the respective Dropbox or Google Docs budget folder right away. Remember that losing receipts means no reimbursement, and therefore it means losing your money (see Figure 2.5).

Sharing Files with Other Collaborators and the Wardrobe Department: Google Docs, Dropbox, etc.

I like to use Dropbox to host and share show folders that contain my up-to-date information. I include contact sheets, measurements, research, finished sketches, etc. in them. I use Google Docs for items in process, i.e., updating a costume plot or a costume

FIGURE 2.3

Sample of costume breakdowns for the musical *Kiss Me Kate* at the Lyric Stage Company of Boston.

Costume Piece List
Page 1

#	ACTOR / DANCER		Costume	CHARACTER (S)		Notes	Laundry and D/C
	Last Name	First Name	Number	Description			
1		Jack		Harry Trevor, Baptista	2 Equity Tshirs - Through out	Buy- LS	W/D
			X1	Actor	Blue Stripe Shirt	Pull- ES	W/D
	Height: 5' 11'				Brown Plaid Jacket	Pull- ES	D/C
	Weight: 175				Brown Plaid Vest	Build- LS	D/C
	Suit: 42 R				Brown Plaid Pants	Build- LS	D/C
	Pants: 34 x 32 or M/L				Straw Hat, Bow Tie, Suspenders	Pull- LS	Spot Clean
	Shirt: 16 x 34 or M/L				2 Prs Socks	Buy- LS	W/D
	Shoes: 9.5 narrow				Black Loafers	Buy- LS	Buff
			X2	Baptista	Beige Chemise Shirt	LS - Build	W/D
					Black Knickers	LS - Build	W/D
					Green/Gold Cape	Pull- ES	D/C
					Green Hose	Pull- ES	W/D
					Black Boots	Buy - LS	Buff
					Damask Cape	Pull- ES	D/C
					Red Collar, Gold Beaded Necklace	Pull- ES	Spot Clean
					Black Hat with Feather	Pull- ES	Spot Clean
			X3	Act II Finale	Fox Fur Stole	Build- LS	Spot Clean
					Patchwork Cape Tunic	Build- LS	D/C

Prepared by Rafael Jaen 9/26/2009

Costume Piece List
Page 2

#	ACTOR / DANCER		Costume	CHARACTER (S)		Notes	Laundry and D/C
	Last Name	First Name	Number	Description			
2		Rachel		Female Dance Ensemble			
			X1	Dancer	Camisole - THROUGHOUT	Buy- LS	W/D
	Height: 5' 2"				Bloomers - THROUGHOUT	Buy- LS	W/D
	Weight: 120				Shaper - THROUGHOUT	Buy- LS	Hand Wash
	Dress: 0-2 Petite				Brown Polka Dot Dress - Take off	Pull- ES	D/C
	Tights: S				Lilac Blouse - AO	Build- LS	D/C
	Bra: 32B				Tan Heels - THROUGHOUT - ACTRESS' OWN		
	Shoes: 6.5				Brown Hat, Brown Gloves, Brown Purse	Pull- LS	Spot Clean
					Bum Roll - AO	Pull- LS	
			X2A	Player I, 4	Red Dress	Pull- LS	D/C
					Crinoline - TAKE OFF FOR 'WE OPEN IN VENICE'	Pull- ES	Spot Clean
					Blue/Brown Veil - TAKE OFF FOR 'WE OPEN IN VENICE'	Build- LS	Spot Clean
			X2B	Player II, 6	X2A		
					Take off Veil		
			X3	Wench I,8	Crinoline	Pull- ES	
					Bum Roll	Pull- LS	
					Lilac Blouse	Build- LS	
					Blue Striped Bodice	Pull- ES	D/C
					Purple Skirt	Build- LS	D/C
					Pink Apron & Purple Hat	Pull- LS	W/D
			X4	Dancer Backstage	Pink Silk Robe	Buy- LS	W/D
			X5	Pavana II, 8	X2A		
					Golden Surcote - AO	Build- LS	D/C
					Golden Headband	Build- LS	Spot Clean

Prepared by Rafael Jaen 9/26/2009

FIGURE 2.4

I include the actor's basic sizes (in case something needs replacing during the run), source (bought, built, or pulled), and wardrobe maintenance (laundry or dry-cleaning) information.

FIGURE 2.5

A sample of a preliminary budget spec. I use them in conjunction with the costume plot in negotiating the final number of costumes. I discuss what the actors are wearing in specific scenes and cut items without sacrificing the storytelling.

Lyric Stage's "Kiss Me Kate" Costume Price Specs

ACTOR AND/OR DANCER	CHARACTER (S)	TOTALS	ITEMS	SPECS			
				Buy	Pull	Build	Labor
1 Arthur w	Pops -Doorman, Padua Priest, Half Donkey	2	UndershirtShirt, Pants, Jacket (Uniform?), Red Cassock, Priest robes and hat, Shoes	$ 10.00	$ -	$ 50.00	$ -
2 Mary C	Hattie - Lilli's Dresser	2	Coat, Hat, Blouse, Skirt, Shoes, Hose	$ 35.00	$ -	$ 50.00	$ -
3 TBA	Paul -Dresser, Ensemble Singer	2	UndershirtShirt, Pants, Jacket, Hat, Vest, Suspemders, Shoes	$ 10.00	$ -	$ -	$ -
4 Phil C	Ralph Stage Manager, Singer, Half Donkey	2	UndershirtShirt, Pants, Jacket, Hat, Vest, Suspemders, Shoes, Donkey	$ 10.00	$ -	$ 50.00	$ -
5 Michele D	Lois Lane -Chanteuse, Bianca	4	Street Clothes, Dance Clothes, 2 Rennaisance Outfits (blouse, vest, skirts, etc)	$ 350.00	$ -	$ 25.00	$ -
6 Patrick R	Bill Calhoun -hoofer, Lucencio	3	UndershirtShirt, Pants, Jacket, Hat, Vest, Suspemders, Shoes, Ren Shirt, 2 Doublets, Stockings, Shoes	$ 350.00	$ -	$ 20.00	$ -
7 Amelia B	Lilli Vanessi -Star, Katharine	6	Dior Outfits, Back Stage Robe, Katahrine Dress, Wedding Outfit, Shoes	$ 500.00	$ -	$ 100.00	$ -
8 TBA	Fred Graham -Producer/Director, Petruchio	4	UndershirtShirt, Pants, Jacket, Hat, Vest, Suspenders, Shoes, Ren Shirts, 2 Doublets, Capes, Stockings, Boots	$ 350.00	$ -	$ 50.00	$ -
9 Jack A	Harry Trevor -Veteran Actor, Baptista	4	UndershirtShirt, Pants, Jacket, Hat, Vest, Suspemders, Shoes, Ren Shirt, 2 Doublets, Stockings, Shoes	$ 250.00	$ -	$ 20.00	$ -
10 Santio C	Stage Hand 1, Musician, Nathaniel -P. Servant	5	UndershirtShirt, Pants, Jacket, Hat, Vest, Suspemders, Shoes, Ren Shirt, 2 Doublets, Stockings, Shoes	$ 250.00	$ -	$ 20.00	$ -
11 Neil C	1st Man -Gunman, Finale Donkey	2	Gangster Suit, shirts, spats, shoes, etc. Rennaisance outifit, tabbards, shirts, pants, hats and wigs --rent donkey	$ 200.00	$ -	$ 35.00	$ -
12 J.T.	2nd Man -Gunman, Finale Donkey	2	Gangster Suit, shirts, spats, shoes, etc. Rennaisance outifit, tabbards, shirts, pants, hats and wigs	$ 200.00	$ -	$ 35.00	$ -
13 Peter M	Flynt -Dancer, Gremio -Suitor	5	UndershirtShirt, Pants, Jacket, Hat, Vest, Suspemders, Shoes, Ren Shirt, 2 Doublets, Stockings, Shoes	$ 250.00	$ -	$ 25.00	$ -
14 Joseph C	Riley -Dancer, motorist, Gen Aide, Hortensio -Suitor	5	UndershirtShirt, Pants, Jacket, Hat, Vest, Suspemders, Shoes, Ren Shirt, 2 Doublets, Stockings, Shoes	$ 300.00	$ -	$ 25.00	$ -
15 Josh D	Stage Hand 2, Cab Driver, Musician, Philip -P. Servant	4	UndershirtShirt, Pants, Jacket, Hat, Vest, Suspemders, Shoes, Ren Shirt, 2 Doublets, Stockings, Shoes	$ 250.00	$ -	$ 20.00	$ -
16 TBA	General Harrison Howell	1	Uniform, shirt, boots, hat, overcoat	$ 300.00	$ -	$ 25.00	$ -
17 Caitlin D	Singer 1 -Bianca's Quartet, Inn Waitress	4	Street Clothes, Dance Clothes, 2 Rennaisance Outfits (blouse, vest, skirts, etc)	$ 250.00	$ -	$ 20.00	$ -
18 Catherine C	Singer 2 -Bianca's Quartet, Inn Waitress	3	Street Clothes, Dance Clothes, 2 Rennaisance Outfits (blouse, vest, skirts, etc)	$ 250.00	$ -	$ 20.00	$ -
19 Hillary W	Singer 3 -Bianca's Quartet, Inn Waitress	3	Street Clothes, Dance Clothes, 2 Rennaisance Outfits (blouse, vest, skirts, etc)	$ 250.00	$ -	$ 20.00	$ -
20 Rachel B	Female Dancer 1	4	Street Clothes, Dance Clothes, 2 Rennaisance Outfits (blouse, vest, skirts, etc)	$ 250.00	$ -	$ 20.00	$ -
21 Shanna H	Female Dancer 2	4	Street Clothes, Dance Clothes, 2 Rennaisance Outfits (blouse, vest, skirts, etc)	$ 250.00	$ -	$ 20.00	$ -
Cutting & Draping			Lilli's Dior, Hattie's Dress, Donkey	$ -	$ -	$ -	$ 1,050.00
Stitchers			Fitting Alterations, Donkey, Hattie's Dress	$ -	$ -	$ -	$ 1,600.00
Wigs & Wig Master			Lois/Bianca wigs; Lilli/Kate wigs = $250 plus miscelaneous millinery	$ 400.00	$ -	$ -	$ 350.00
			SUB-TOTAL $	$ 5,265.00	$ -	$ 650.00	$ 3,000.00
		71	TOTAL	$			8,915.00

Notes: _____

_____

_____

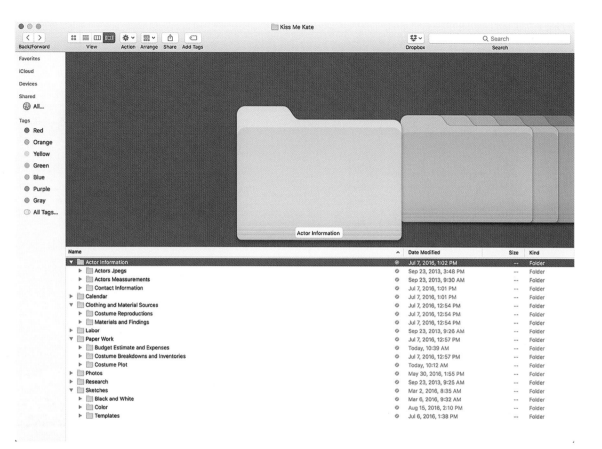

FIGURE 2.6

A sample of a digital folder in Google Docs. I save all the information digitally via spreadsheets, Word documents, JPEGs, etc.

piece list—also known as a breakdown or an inventory (see Figure 2.6).

I also take photos of the actors during fittings and upload them in a Flickr folder so the director and the team can see the progress and offer notes before tech/dress (see Figures 2.7 and 2.8).

Finally, to quote the HubPages site,

Creating a bible may seem like a waste of energy but I can't stress enough how helpful it is. Designing a show is stressful, and sometimes you can get distracted or confused. But by being organized and keeping everything you need to know in one binder, you minimize the amount of time spent looking things up and can just focus on what you need to do.[3]

FIGURE 2.7

A sample of a Flickr folder for the musical *Kiss Me Kate* at the Lyric Stage Company of Boston. I took fitting photos and saved them into the show album, adding research information for the director to read.

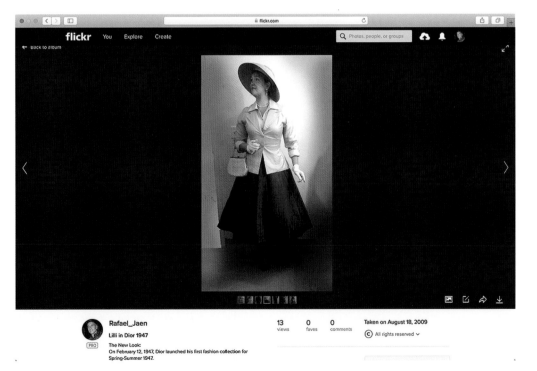

FIGURE 2.8

Figure 2.8 features award-winning actress Amelia Broome. I added a description of the Christian Dior's New Look from the website: www.dior.com/couture/en_us/the-house-of-dior/the-story-of-dior/the-new-look-revolution

Digital Costume Design Studio

A Digital Costume Design Studio is a creative space for the production of two-dimensional projects, e.g., a costume sketch that will eventually come to life appearing on stage or film. It would include digital equipment, software, and archival systems. These would be cloud-based (online) file-sharing systems that allow the user to draw, read, and write over the Internet.

Digital Studio Basics

A digital studio requires some minimal equipment including a computer or laptop, sketching software, a drawing tablet, a current cellular phone, and an all-in-one (print/scan/copy) wirelessly activated (Bluetooth) printer. It will also need a large amount of online (cloud) memory. All of the equipment can be networked via online (cloud) sharing so your files can be accessed from any of your devices.

If you need help setting up your network, seek out assistance from IT personnel or a knowledgeable colleague.

File-Sharing Options

I recommend using various cloud-based (online) file-sharing options, including Dropbox, Google Docs, Pinterest, and Flickr. The more projects, the more memory a designer will need to use, so there may be some worthwhile (business expense) costs associated with using these digital platforms.

1. "**Dropbox** is a home for all your photos, docs, videos, and files. Anything you add to Dropbox will automatically show up on all your computers, phones and even the Dropbox website—so you can access your stuff from anywhere." It works like any other folder on your hard drive, with an advantage: the files you drag into your Dropbox folder automatically sync online and to any other computers or mobile devices linked to your account.[4] There is a helpful YouTube tutorial at www.youtube.com/watch?v=29qfd5zDU8A.

2. "**Google Docs**, Sheets, and Slides are productivity apps that let you create different kinds of online documents, work on them in real time with other people, and store them in your Google Drive online—all for free. You can access the documents, spreadsheets, and presentations you create from any computer, anywhere in the world. There's even some work you can do without an Internet connection!"[5] (see Figure 2.9). There is a helpful YouTube tutorial at www.youtube.com/watch?v=CeFJvXhFJd8.

3. "**Pinterest** is a social network that allows users to visually share and discover new interests by posting (known as 'pinning' on Pinterest) images or videos to their own or others' boards (i.e., a collection of 'pins,' usually with a common theme) and browsing what other users have pinned." "Users can either upload images from their computer or pin things they find on the web using the Pinterest bookmarklet (or pinit button)."[6] This is very useful when saving research (pins) for a show; one can include shopping sources, book sources, etc. with each image. There is a helpful YouTube tutorial at www.youtube.com/watch?v=hds8J6Gtxk4.

4. **Flickr** (pronounced "flicker") is an image hosting website and Web services suite that was acquired by Yahoo in 2005. "In Flickr, you can give your friends, family, and other contacts permission to organize your stuff – not just to add comments, but also notes and tags."[7] There is a helpful YouTube tutorial at www.youtube.com/watch?v=hJ3adutZpPw.

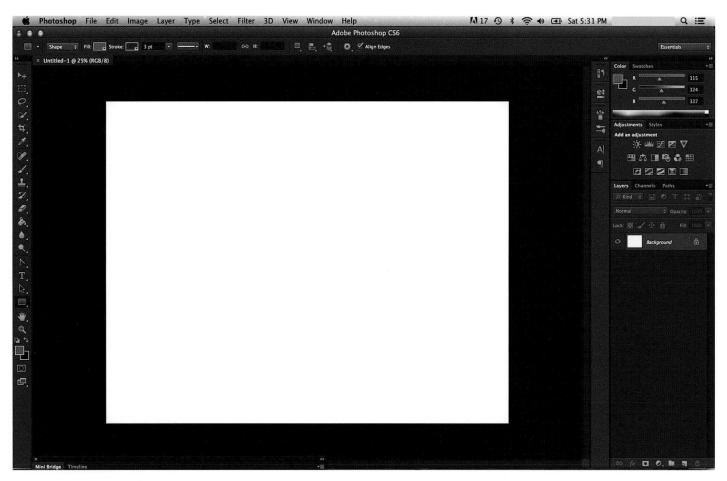

FIGURE 2.9

The Photoshop screen is a digital version of the traditional artist caddy.

Drawing Tablets and Digital Rendering Software

Using drawing tablets reminds me of using my sketchpad in life figure drawing classes. It takes the same visual and kinesthetic skills. It also reminds me of using the right pressure with my pencil when I draw free hand. Digital rendering reminds me of different media such as watercolor's transparency, acrylic's opacity, and design markers' blending. In this chapter, I am sharing some insights about the equipment and software that I use. There are other options in the market, but the ones described in this book are my favorites.

Wacom Tablets

Let's get our definitions straight here, folks: Unlike the iPad, the Kindle Fire or the Nook, Wacom tablets are not your average tablet PCs. Nor do they strive to be—they're graphics tablets (also called pen tablets), devices used in the graphic design industry or by digital artists that allow a person to draw by hand, capturing an image or graphic in digital form. The information is displayed on the monitor of a connected PC or Mac.[8]

A Wacom tablet is a type of input device for a computer that is extremely useful for costume designers. It is more intuitive than using a mouse and keyboard, and it makes editing or touching-up drawings less time consuming. It feels as natural as a pen or brush. Wacom is a very well-known professional brand that produces touch-sensitive graphics tablets. I love using it at my studio as well as in the classroom; the company offers different models at every price range. There are many helpful tutorials online that teach how to make the most of your tablet's pen and touch features. I favor the YouTube tutorial Getting Started with Intuos 2015: Using Pen and Touch. "Learn how to get started with your new Intuos in this tutorial explaining how to make the most of your tablet's pen and touch features."[9]

Photoshop

Photoshop is Adobe's photo editing, image creation, and graphic design software. . . . It uses a layer-based editing system that enables image creation and altering with multiple overlays that support transparency. Layers can also act as masks or filters, altering underlying colors. Shadows and other effects can be added to the layers (Figure 2.9).[10]

Photoshop has become an industry standard, and its name a verb. It is common parlance to say that an image has been "photoshopped" or altered. Many professionals use this software, including photographers, graphic designers, video game artists, and advertising and meme designers. Fashion and costume designers use it as well. The software is available for a monthly fee,

FIGURE 2.10
A traditional (Utrecht) side desk caddy.

depending on the user's requirements. Photoshop CC is compatible with Intel-based Mac computers and Windows PCs as well. I look at the Photoshop screen as if it were my drafting table. It has its own "caddy" with all the necessary tools organized in a specific way, including some that I may re-discover now and then! (See Figure 2.10.)

Basic Digital Rendering Tools

The Photoshop screen contains left interface columns and upper interface rows, with various options and dialogue windows. Usually, you can find essential tools such as Brush, Eraser, and Paint Bucket on the left side interface column. There are also various modalities on the upper interface row, including Dissolve, Burn, and Dodge. These applications can be very useful when rendering costumes. They easily translate to painting with watercolors, design markers, or acrylic paints. Additionally, there are dialogue windows on the right interface columns that show Layers, Color Swatches, and History.

In the next few chapters, we'll become familiar with these various tools; the important matter is to understand the Photoshop screen as if it were a drafting table with many drawing and painting supplies.

Below are brief descriptions of the useful tools that we will use in the next chapters.

1. **Layers:** I think of them as a stack of tracing paper or acetate sheets. You can control their transparency to see what's below, and you can move them into a different order within a stack. I usually draw each clothing item on a separate layer, so I can isolate changes rather than having to redo a whole sketch. For instance, I can turn a red skirt into a green version for a director to see the difference without impacting the rest of the costume sketch.

2. **Levels and Curves:** These are photo editing tools, but we can use them to adjust black & white drawings before painting. By adjusting brightness and contrast, we can obtain better tonality and clearer silhouette outlines.

3. **Flatting:** The consolidation (or merging) of multiple layers into one.

4. **Brushes (and Pencils):** Photoshop contains dialogue windows with various brush options; you can also create your own and save them for future drawings.

5. **Burn and Dodge:** These tools can lighten or darken areas of the rendering. They are based on traditional darkroom techniques for regulating exposure within specific areas of a print. I think of Burn as a "tanning" and Dodge as a "bleaching" method (see Figure 2.11).

6. **Dissolve:** This is a blended modality that creates a "speckled" pattern when painting.

7. **Patterns:** These are layer "fills" and overlays. They are part of the Paint Bucket tool presets. For costume renderings, they can be used to create or reproduce fabric patterns.

8. **Fonts:** Photoshop contains a Font tool with different styles containing letters, numbers, and symbols. They can be utilized as a layer to add titles and notations to sketches.

9. **Special Effects:** The software has many effects that I use to manipulate the final image. The main ones are Bevel, Emboss, and Inner and Outer Shadows. I use these effects to add outline shadows and highlights to separate the costume silhouette from its background. It is a quick and easy way to add dimension to your drawing.

FIGURE 2.11

My costume sketch for Lili, in *Kiss Me Kate,* Act I, Scene 1. I used the Burn and Dodge modalities to add a painterly effect to the sketch.

LILLI
Act I,1

Other Resources: Free Croquis

A fashion croquis is an outline sketch of a figure model in various poses. The apparel industry uses them as drawing templates for sketching design ideas. "Traditionally, a fashion croquis figure is nine heads tall, but this can vary depending on the designer's aesthetics. Fashion figures are traditionally slender with exaggerated long legs."[11] Nowadays, many free sources on the Internet provide a variety of male and female croquis in different poses; they also include plus sizes and children.

I recommend creating a resource folder that contains a collection of croquis. They would include your own black & white (scanned) silhouette drawings, free downloaded croquis, and actual full-body fashion photos. Having a collection will help when planning to illustrate any particular garment (see Figure 2.12).

Testimonial

SPIRO VELOUDOS, PRODUCING ARTISTIC DIRECTOR AND THEATRE
DIRECTOR

My primary job is to serve the playwright by telling his/her story.

Bio
Spiro Veloudos, now in his eighteenth season as Producing Artistic Director of the Lyric Stage, has recently directed *Sweeney Todd*, *Into the Woods* (Elliot Norton Awards for Best Director and Outstanding Musical Production), *One Man*, *Two Guvnors*, and *Death of a Salesman*. In previous seasons he directed *The Mikado*, *33 Variations*, *On the Town*, *Avenue Q* (Elliot Norton Awards for Outstanding Musical and Outstanding Ensemble, five IRNE Awards including Best Musical and Best Director), *The Life and Adventures of Nicholas Nickleby* (Elliot Norton Awards for Best Production and Best Director, five IRNE Awards including Best

FIGURE 2.12

A sample of various free-download fashion croquis. I use them as a base and draw over them with transparent Photoshop layers as if they were tracing paper.

Judith Bliss   Myra   Clara   Jackie   Sorel Bliss

Director), *Big River*, *Superior Donuts*, *Animal Crackers*, *Blithe Spirit*, *Lady Day at Emerson's Bar & Grill*, and *Kiss Me Kate*. Spiro received the Lifetime Achievement in the Arts Award from Salem State College. He was the recipient of the 2006 Elliot Norton Prize for Sustained Excellence. During his tenure, the Lyric Stage has earned numerous awards and honors including Elliot Norton Awards for Outstanding Production (*Into the Woods*, *Nicholas Nickleby*, *Speech & Debate*, *Miss Witherspoon*, *The Old Settler*), and Outstanding Musical Production (*Into the Woods*, *Sunday in the Park with George*); Independent Reviewers of New England (IRNE) Awards for Outstanding Production (*Nicholas Nickleby*, *The Old Settler*, *Glengarry Glen Ross*), and Outstanding Musical Production (*Grey Gardens*, *Urinetown: The Musical*, *A Little Night Music*, *Sunday in the Park with George*). His numerous directing credits at the Lyric Stage include *A Little Night Music* (IRNE Award for Direction), *Glengarry Glen Ross* (IRNE Award), *Sunday in the Park with George* (Best of the Year in Boston's Globe, Herald, and Phoenix; Elliot Norton and IRNE Award for direction), *Assassins* (Best Production of 1998: The Boston Globe), *Lost in Yonkers*, *Never the Sinner: The Leopold and Loeb Story* (Elliot Norton Award, along with Assassins), and *Speed-the-Plow* (Elliot Norton for Outstanding Production). Mr. Veloudos received StageSource's Theatre Hero Award (2003) and was named Best Artistic Director by *Boston Magazine* in 1999. He serves as the president for the Producers' Association of New England Area Theatres, and is adjunct faculty in Performing Arts at Emerson College.[12]

Interview

Rafael: In your experience, what makes for an effective theatre collaboration?

Spiro: Trust, listening, and having a clear vision to impart to your collaborators.

Rafael: What is your role in telling the story?

Spiro: I think of the director as the chief storyteller; my primary job is to serve the playwright by telling his/her story.

Rafael: What are your thoughts about collaborating with designers; what do you look for?

Spiro: I like designers that bring their own ideas to the table. I don't like to re-create a production. So it's incumbent on the design team to take my verbal description on the play and create a visual context for it. The designers create the world of the play. I work within that world.

Rafael: In today's digital era, what are some of the things that you find helpful when communicating with designers via the World Wide Web?

Spiro: I'm an old dog. I have issues with communicating digitally. However, having art, music, pictures, and images available, on demand, makes design meetings more efficient. Having cloud-based storage, like Dropbox, makes having preliminary or final designs accessible. It also helps in communicating between the design team, which makes for an effective collaborative effort.

Rafael: What advice would you give a young theatre practitioner who is starting to work professionally?

Spiro: Don't assume you stop learning after a training program. You must stay open to new ideas and practices. Learn from your mistakes. Don't be afraid of failure. But, learn from the failure. Don't do the same thing again thinking the result will be different.

Design Gallery: *Sweeney Todd*

Stephen Sondheim's Tony-Award-winning *Sweeney Todd*, a macabre musical thriller, blends Sondheim's characteristic wit with a sweeping and hauntingly beautiful score, grisly humor, and chilling drama. Set against the backdrop of the shadowy back alleys and side streets of 19th-century London, the musical follows disgraced barber Sweeney Todd on his quest for vengeance after years of unjust imprisonment and exile. With the aid of Mrs. Lovett, the proprietor of a failing pie shop, Sweeney sets out to avenge the terrible wrongs done to him and his family.[13]

FIGURE 2.13

Production photo for *Sweeney Todd*, Act I; featuring actors Amelia Broome (Mrs. Lovett) and Christopher Chew (Sweeney) in the main roles.

FIGURE 2.14

Costume color palette for *Sweeney Todd*, Lyric Stage Company of Boston, Fall 2014.

FIGURE 2.15

Costume sketch for Mrs. Lovett (Costume #1), *Sweeney Todd*, Lyric Stage Company of Boston, Fall 2014. For this sketch I used a free croquis as my base, and I resized it to be 9" tall in a 11.5" wide x 17" tall sheet.

FIGURE 2.16

Costume sketch for Sweeney Todd (Costume #1), *Sweeney Todd,* Lyric Stage Company of Boston, Fall 2014. For this sketch I used a free croquis as my base, and I resized it to be 9" tall in a 11.5" wide x 17" tall sheet.

FIGURE 2.17

Costume sketch for Mrs. Lovett (Costume #3), *Sweeney Todd,* Lyric Stage Company of Boston, Fall 2014. For this sketch I used a free croquis as my base, and I resized it to be 9" tall in a 11.5" wide x 17" tall sheet.

FIGURE 2.18

Production photo for *Sweeney Todd*, Act I; featuring actors Amelia Broome (Mrs. Lovett) and Christopher Chew (Sweeney) in the main roles.

Citations and Sources

1   "About Us." The Lyric Stage Company of Boston. Accessed August 27, 2016. www.lyricstage.com/about/staff.cfm.

2   "Creating a Costume Bible." HubPages. November 19, 2009. Accessed July 06, 2016. http://hubpages.com/education/Creating-a-Costume-Bible.

3   "Creating a Costume Bible." HubPages. November 19, 2009. Accessed July 06, 2016. http://hubpages.com/education/Creating-a-Costume-Bible.

4   "Dropbox—Tour." Dropbox. Accessed July 07, 2016. www.dropbox.com/tour.

5   "Overview of Google Docs, Sheets, and Slides." Docs Editors Help. Accessed July 07, 2016. https://support.google.com/docs/answer/49008?hl=en.

6   "What Is Pinterest, and How Does It Work?" Accessed July 07, 2016. www.infront.com/blogs/the-infront-blog/2014/1/20/what-is-pinterest-and-how-does-it-work.

7   Flickr. Accessed July 07, 2016. www.flickr.com/about.

8   Kershner, Kate. "How Wacom Tablets Work." HowStuffWorks. 2012. Accessed July 07, 2016. http://computer.howstuffworks.com/tablets/wacom-tablets.htm.

9   Wacom. "Getting Started with Intuos 2015: Using Pen and Touch." YouTube. 2015. Accessed July 07, 2016."www.youtube.com/watch?v=gXBt9XImEL0.

10   "What Is Photoshop? Definition from WhatIs.com." WhatIs.com. Accessed July 07, 2016. http://whatis.techtarget.com/definition/Photoshop.

11   "Free Fashion Croquis: 120 Fashion Figure Templates." Designers Nexus. Accessed July 07, 2016. www.designersnexus.com/fashion-design-portfolio/fashion-design-croquis-template/.

12   "About Us." The Lyric Stage Company of Boston. Accessed August 27, 2016. www.lyricstage.com/about/staff.cfm.

13   "Sweeney Todd." The Lyric Stage of Boston. Accessed September 01, 2016. www.lyricstage.com/productions/production.cfm?ID=82.

A DIRECTOR IS TOTALLY RESPONSIBLE FOR THE CULTURE OF THEIR

PRODUCTION – WHETHER IT IS DISCIPLINED OR LAZY, RESTRICTIVE

OR FREEING, A JOYFUL OR A STRESSFUL PLACE.

CARRIE ANN QUINN, ACTOR AND DIRECTOR

CHAPTER 3

DRAWING THE CHARACTER'S SPINE; BLACK & WHITE DRAWING BASICS

FIGURE 3.1

Sample of Rafael Jaen's finished sketch for *The Mikado*, produced at the Lyric Stage Company of Boston, 2012. The finished sketch depicts a happy (smiling), bright (color), and jumping (dancing) character.

Costume designers' first sketches are usually "rough" black & white line drawings. These renderings need to define the characters' spines; meaning their particular stand, physical attributes, and gestures. I also like taking into consideration the subject's emotions, qualities, and actions. For example, when drawing a happy (smiling), shining (bright color), and jumping (dancing) individual, designers would choose an image that is compatible with these ideas (see Figure 3.1).

I will share different rendering techniques for this first step, including drawing "rough" line figures on a vellum pad and then scanning them to my computer and drawing (freehand) shapes digitally, using a Wacom tablet. Sometimes I also trace a pre-existing JPEG image or a croquis downloaded from the Web.

Scanning and/or Copying Black & White Drawings

With a scanner, designers can quickly convert paper drawings to searchable PDF files for easy email distribution and review, and for archival purposes. PDF files are especially useful in the digital design process for two reasons: 1) all types of documents can be easily SAVED and sized as PDF files; and 2) PDF files can also be SAVED as JPEG images for slideshows. Another function that is useful is the copying and duplicating of images before editing, not just in Photoshop but also when using images via different file-sharing platforms such as Dropbox. I always recommend having duplicates of original drawings in case a file gets corrupted or when an editing change can't be undone.

Scanning Steps and Tips

1. Make sure that the scanner is installed and recognized by the user's computer and that it is connected via a USB port or Bluetooth.

2. Become familiar with your home and your office scanners; the prompts may vary depending on the brand.

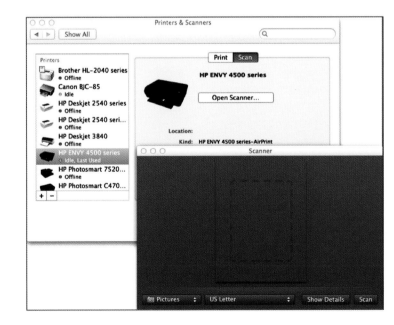

FIGURE 3.2

Become familiar with your scanners; the prompts may vary depending on the brand.

3. Choose Create or Scan and SAVE the intended drawing file as a PDF.

4. Additionally, select "Color Image" in the document presets when prompted. This step will help you later when re-saving the image as a JPEG (or TIFF) for painting in Photoshop.

5. Users may be able to press the "Scan" button on their printer, and then choose Adobe Acrobat from the list of registered applications that appear on the interface window in the prompting computer screen.

6. A scanned PDF file image can be reduced (for email) by choosing: View > Tools > Document Processing, then "Optimize" under Tools. The window prompters will offer options for the size of document. Optimization options are described in detail in Acrobat Help.[1]

7. Finally, always remember to SAVE the PDF file as a JPEG image so it can be painted with Photoshop later.

Tracing with the Wacom Tablet

Tracing with a Wacom tablet can feel challenging, yet remember that practice always makes perfect. It is about training the eye/hand coordination to execute shapes using surfaces (screens) with different orientations, and it is not that different from live figure drawing.

Here are some basics that may assist designers when practicing:

1. Make sure the proper Wacom tablet software is installed on the computer that you are using—especially if you alternate between work and home. It varies from model to model.

2. Get an idea of your bearings by moving the stylus cursor around; it will work as a mouse. There is usually a default setting that matches the rectangle of your computer screen, so you may not need to make changes at the start.

3. To start drawing in Photoshop, create a "New," size 11x17 document and practice drawing doodles, squares, round shapes, etc.

4. Find your "drawing hand," e.g., draw by holding the stylus in the same manner that you grab your pen or pencil. While some designers may prefer holding the pen close to the black nib tip, others may like to grab it above the side control bar.

5. Practice tracing over various existing images to train your eye/hand coordination.

Tracing Over Existing Images: A Sample Process

What is a croquis? It is a rough preliminary drawing. The word is equivalent to the French *croqu(er)*, or to make a quick sketch of, or a rough out.[2]

Using Fashion Croquis

A fashion croquis is a line sketch of a figure (model) in various illustration poses, which fashion designers use as a drawing template for sketching apparel design ideas. Traditionally, a fashion croquis figure is nine to ten heads tall; this size can be too tall for a costume sketch. Additionally, fashion figures are usually slender with exaggerated long legs, so they would need to be resized (transformed) for costume silhouettes.[3]

In this chapter I am using the term "croquis" in more general terms, referring to a pre-existing (or rough preliminary) silhouette that a designer would use to draw costume ideas.

Using a Pre-Existing Image

Steps

Below are the steps of a tracing that took place prior to executing the final sketch seen in Figure 3.1.

1. Open a new 11x17 Photoshop document: FILE > NEW DOCUMENT, then specify 11 width x 17 height in the interface window (see Figure 3.3).

2. While in Photoshop, open a JPEG of body type that you want to use as your base (I am calling it CROQUIS). Copy the image and then paste it in your original new document. In the sample, I did IMAGE > ROTATION > 30 DEGREES to get the movement that looked similar to what the choreographer described (see Figure 3.4).

3. Duplicate the image LAYER, then hit MAGIC-WAND > SELECT > INVERSE and paint it white using a wide brush with white paint so it becomes a white sheet.

4. Set it at 50–55% Opacity on the upper side options of your LAYERS interface dialogue box so it becomes a semi-transparent sheet (see Figure 3.5).

5. Now you can trace the silhouette to create your B & W layer, keeping continuous lines; in this case I drew the specific costume that I researched and I was hoping to either buy or build.

FIGURE 3.3

Opening a new 11x17 Photoshop document.

FIGURE 3.4

While in Photoshop, open a JPEG of body type that you want to use as your base. In this case I am using a figure from the online vendor source www.china-cart.com.

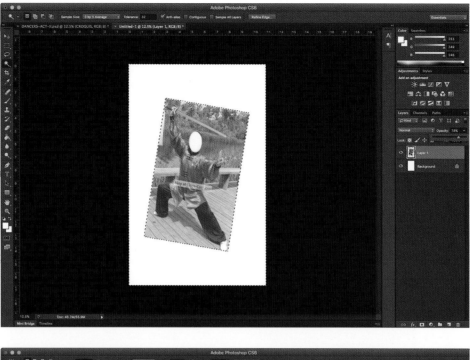

FIGURE 3.5

Set layers at 50–55% Opacity so they become semi-transparent for tracing.

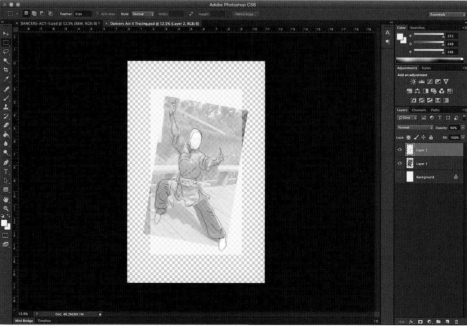

FIGURE 3.6

The final black & white drawing after
tracing the pre-chosen JPEG image.

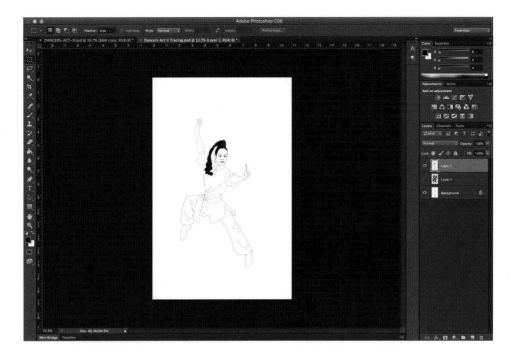

6. You can add new layers, too; for example, I
   duplicated the B & W Silhouette layer and erased
   everything but the face to draw it separately—there
   was a chance that the brunette dancer would be
   recast with a blond one (see Figure 3.6).

7. The next step would be the creation of the
   background template and the painting of the various
   layers (hiding the CROQUIS layer). Tracing, in this
   case, becomes a skill-building tool.

8. I also like to add a layer with the actor's face
   (headshot); I trace it and add it to my final croquis.
   I also take into consideration the actor's height
   and weight or body type; in this way I can draw a
   character that will accurately reflect the actor's body
   and costume silhouette in my sketch.

Creating a "Croquis Bank"

Since I started to use and create croquis, I have been
saving them in a folder in Dropbox. I now have a bank
of each of them as black & white drawings, which I can
re-use as a base. This strategy helps me SAVE time and
keeps me practicing my digital drawing skills.

Preparing and Saving Black & White Images for Painting with Photoshop

For best results, it is necessary to SAVE images with fine
and clear lines. Designers can easily achieve this step
by adjusting the picture's levels and the contrast, and by
cleaning the background (see Figure 3.7).

Preparing Black & White Drawings[4]

Below are the comprehensive steps that will help
you prepare a black & white image for painting with

FIGURE 3.7

Photoshop. They match the ones depicted in my YouTube channel: www.youtube.com/user/JaenRafael/videos (see Figure 3.8).

Steps

1. Open scanned image. In the case of the example, it is a TIFF file.

2. If the image is far off center, you can use the Marquee tool to outline the borders you would like, and then crop away the rest by clicking [Image] > [Crop].

3. Change size by pressing [Image] > [Image Size], and then raising the resolution of the scanned image.

4. Zoom out until image fits the screen by pressing [Command] > [-].

5. Go to [Image] > [Adjustments] > [Levels . . .], slide the changeable darkness-leveler to slightly past the midpoint of the scale, and lower the lightness-leveler down slightly, just to clear the background—this will also thin the lines slightly (see Figure 3.9).

6. SAVE into a folder that will exclusively hold your B & W line drawings for your show.

7. In the "layer" toolbar, duplicate the line drawing image that you are working on, and name the copy Silhouette.

8. Click the left Eye icon to hide Layer "0."

9. Select the Magic Wand tool.

10. Click on the background. A flickering dotted line should appear around your character's image. If

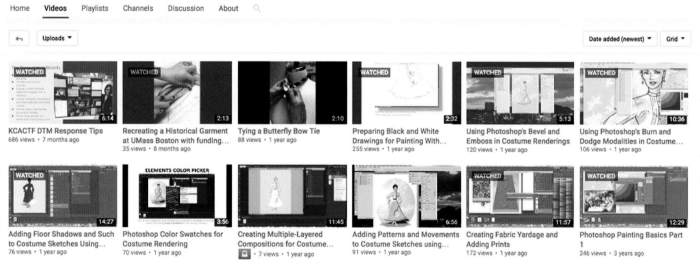

FIGURE 3.8

Rafael Jaen YouTube channel: www.youtube.com/user/JaenRafael, contains various Photoshop tutorials.

FIGURE 3.9

Go to [Image] > [Adjustments] >
[Levels...], slide the changeable
darkness-leveler to slightly past the
midpoint of the scale, and lower the
lightness-leveler down slightly, just to clear
the background—this will also thin the
lines slightly.

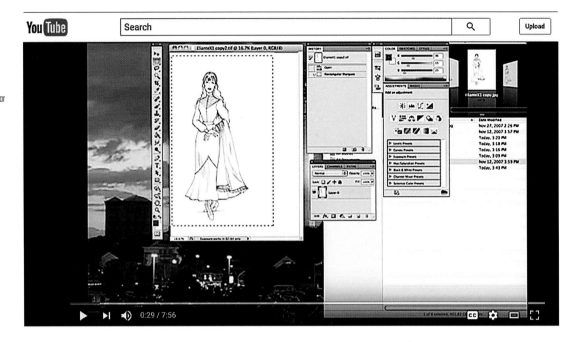

FIGURE 3.10

After deleting the background, you may
now find that you have accidentally
deleted an area you meant to keep—
which means you did in fact have
leakage!

the outline enters the inside of the drawing, then you have to take time to find and close what I call the opening "leakages." These refer to breaks in the drawn lines, and even a tiny one can cause the leakage.

11. Delete the background. You may now find that you have accidentally deleted an area you meant to keep—which means you did in fact have leakage! (See Figure 3.10.)

12. Undo the delete.

13. Zoom in by pressing [Command] > [+].

14. Select the Eyedropper tool.

15. Sample the line color of your black & white drawing.

16. Switch to the Brush tool, set the Opacity to 100%, and make it very fine or thin.

17. Fill in the leakage by closing (joining) any breaks in the actual line of your drawing.

18. Zoom back out so you can see the entire image.

19. Re-select Magic Wand.

20. Select the background, and erase it. If the line in your drawing is complete, no leakage remains; continue forward with the following steps.

21. Now, select other background areas that may have escaped the original delete (maybe they're tucked away from the original background, between the arms and the body, or elsewhere). Erase them. You can select multiple areas by holding [Shift] while you left-click the regions that you want to erase.

22. Press "Enter" or select the Marquee tool, and click elsewhere on the sketch to stop the Magic Wand function and to SAVE the line drawing.

23. Create a New Document.

24. Name it "[Character Name] Color 1."

25. Switch back to the Silhouette image document (your black & white line drawing).

26. Select Magic Wand.

27. Select the background.

28. Go to [Select] > [Inverse]. This is an easy way to select the actual image for copying instead of the background.

29. Copy the image.

30. Paste the Silhouette image into your new document.

31. To make your Silhouette image larger, go to [Image] > [Free Transform]. Now you are able to fit and center your character better in the page. Remember to hold the [Shift] button when using free transform to keep the image proportional; otherwise it may get distorted.

32. SAVE.

33. You now have a white Background layer, and a separate Silhouette layer.

34. Double-check: Go under [Image] > [Mode] and make sure that [RGB] color is selected. If it is not selected, you will not be able to paint the SAVED image.

Inserting Black & White Sketches on Templates[5]

Steps

1. Open Background Template, and B & W drawing. Please be aware that you will have two opened documents in the Photoshop window. They will show in narrow horizontal tabs at the top of the drawing area or as tiny images in a lower interface window.

2. Copy B & W drawing and paste into the open template.

3. Fix image (see Figure 3.11).

   a. Go to: [Image] > [Transform] > [Free Transform].

   b. Drag corners for placement and sizing.

   c. Change height and width of B & W image with the upper interface.

4. Drag and resize image until template and image fit on screen. When done, click the checkmark on the lower right.

5. Choose the Magic Wand from the left side interface (see Figure 3.12).

6. Click on white backgrounds, and delete them.

7. Remember to delete smaller, isolated sections of background area.

8. SAVE the finished B & W image as a Photoshop file.

Fixing Line "Leakages"[6]

When the picture lines in a figure drawing have breaks, they will allow color leakages when painting the costume sketch. It is important to fix these line breaks prior to painting the costume sketch or the paint color will behave like water getting into a boat through a small hole.

Steps

1. If you find an area with leakage, pinpoint the missing boundary.

2. Use Brush or Pencil tool to close lines. Be sure to match the image's line and color (the color palette is found in the bottom left interface, while the drawing tool's line weights are on the upper interface).

3. After the leakages are repaired, re-select Magic Wand tool and continue to delete the white background.

4. Remember to delete smaller, isolated sections of background area.

5. SAVE the finished black & white line drawing as a Photoshop file.

How to Make a 300 to 600 Dpi File

If you open your file in Photoshop and then go to the menu bar Image > Image Size, you will bring up the Image Size dialogue box for the selected open image file. You can change the size and resolution without damaging the file within this box. Notice that changing one setting makes the width and height change as well in proportion. Setting the resolution on 300 (or 600 as you please) you can see the largest size that file can be reproduced at, in its current form. If the resulting dimensions are too small you have the option of making the image a larger dpi or entering the actual width and height that you want.

Testimonial

CARRIE ANN QUINN—ACTOR AND DIRECTOR

The most important premise for me to begin with is the story we are telling onstage — and as a theatre director I am an investigator first.

Bio

Carrie Ann Quinn is a professional actor and director in theatre, television, and film and is a founding member of the international theatre company Escape Artists. She is a proud member of Actor's Equity Association (AEA) and Screen Actors Guild-American Federation of Television and Radio Artists (SAG-AFTRA). Internationally, Professor Quinn recently debuted as an actor and playwright in *Possessions* at the King Street Theatre in Sydney, Australia, a play she co-wrote and toured from its world premiere at Boston Playwrights' Theatre

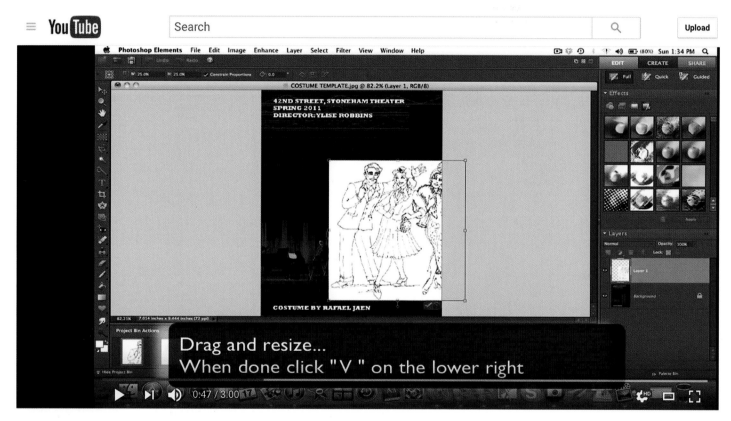

FIGURE 3.11

Fixing the image. Go to: [Image or Edit] > [Transform] > [Free Transform].

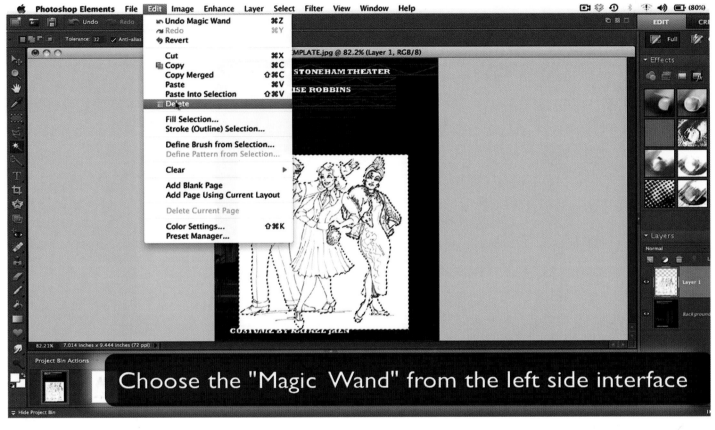

FIGURE 3.12

Using the Magic Wand from the left side interface. Click on the white background and delete it.

to its international premiere in Australia. Professor Quinn's New York theatre credits include plays at the Clurman Theatre Off-Broadway, CSV Flamboyan, New Ohio Theatre, Strasberg Theatre, and other downtown NYC theatre venues. Regional theatre credits include *The Communist Dracula Pageant* (American Repertory Theater/A.R.T.), *An Ideal Husband* (Gloucester Stage Company), *Aurora Borealis* (Huntington's BU Theatre), *The Hothouse* (Huntington Studio 210 Theatre), *Christmas Belles* (Boston Playwrights' Theatre), *Frankie and Johnny in the Clare de Lune* (the Warehouse Theatre), and *The Water Closet* (Whitmore-Lindley Theatre), and as a resident company member for seven years at Theatre Unlimited in Los Angeles, in plays such as *Seven Keys to Baldpate*, *The Ceramic Cow*, *Move Over, Mrs. Markham*, and *The Keys to the Kingdom*. Her professional directing credits include plays produced at Boston Playwrights' Theatre, Chicago's Chopin Theatre, and CenterStage SC. Quinn has appeared and guest starred in film and TV shows for over 20 years, such as *Fame LA*, *Standing By*, *The Fighter*, and *Company Men*, and in numerous independent films, including the recent short film *The Poet*, which she executive produced. Professor Quinn presents her acting technique, Method for a New Millennium, throughout the U.S. and internationally, and works with the Kennedy Center American College Theatre Festival (KCACTF) as a production respondent and Irene Ryan Acting Scholarship coach and judge. Through UMass Boston's affiliation with KCACTF, many Boston students have received regional and national recognition for their acting, design, and dramaturgy work in theatre. At UMass Boston, Quinn has directed Performing Arts Department mainstage shows including *Polaroid Stories* (KCACTF Merit Mention in Directing), *Urinetown The Musical*, *The 25th Annual Putnam County Spelling Bee*, the devised work *Wit? Or Without You!*, *Hedda Gabler*, and *The Shape of Things*.[7]

Interview

Rafael: How would you define your role as a theatre director?

Carrie Ann: I think the role of a theatre director changes with every play: expands, contracts, diverges into new areas. The most important premise for me to begin with is the story we are telling onstage—and as a theatre director I am an investigator first. Researching the history, characters, social/political/ethical issues of the world of the play, and how they connect to the world(s) of the audience. Once the ensemble is cast and I am working with the actors and creative team, I ask lots of questions. A theatre director must challenge their actors, but also support them with a totally safe and freeing environment. A director is totally responsible for the culture of their production—whether it is disciplined or lazy, restrictive or freeing, a joyful or a stressful place. I strive to create, and model myself on, a hard-working and disciplined environment that supports creative freedom, generosity of spirit, and human connection.

Rafael: What is your mantra in regards to theatre collaboration?

Carrie Ann: "Collaborare," Latin definition: "to work together." (Sorry, I'm a Latin/word origin geek.) My mantra for theatre collaboration is that we will work it out *together*—no one is alone. Sometimes one team member needs more help than another, and that is okay—it is not a competition. Everyone is working together on the same goal. Succeed together. Fail together. This is true with the creative team of designers as well as the actor ensemble. Sometimes even more important to reinforce with young actors—student actors. They are introduced to theatre with the audition and casting process, which unfortunately communicates a competitive aspect to theatre. "Competitio," Latin definition: "rivalry." In the beginning rehearsals, the first thing I spend time on is creating the ensemble—and that means transferring any feelings of rivalry that may have developed among the actors into feelings of collaboration.

Rafael: What do you look for when collaborating with designers?

Carrie Ann: I love designers who both share and challenge my visions and ideas. And in the university setting, designers who model the hard work ethic and generosity of spirit I mentioned before. As I wrote above—the director can set a tone, a culture, for a production. I love designers who are investigators themselves—researching and delving into the depths of a story and characters from their own design medium. It is an exciting moment when a director and designers can share their own unique perspectives and yet still forge a unified concept that everyone still feels is their own.

Rafael: What do you look for when collaborating with a costume designer?

Carrie Ann: I love costume designers who love actors. It seems silly to say, but I think great artists must have a healthy appreciation for their medium, right? Sculptors love clay, Painters love paint . . . Thus, costume designers need to love actors and want to "create" the character with them in a loving way. I love costume designers who ask questions—of themselves, their team, the actors, and of me. I love costume designers (and all designers) that surprise me with something I had not thought of!

Rafael: What are your thoughts regarding the use of digital files such as Google Docs, Dropbox, Renderings, etc. as part of the collaborative design-tech process?

Carrie Ann: I love the new digital ways we can share the design-tech process with the team. It makes collaboration easier and makes it better. It allows for directors and designers to really spend time with ideas before committing to them . . . and help avoid spending unnecessary time and money building things that end up not being needed.

The model below demonstrates Director Quinn's investigative approach. She always shares a series of notes that helps define "the story we are telling onstage." As a designer, I find her approach very useful given that it complements my Chapter 1 "Nuts and Bolts" process.

Director's Concept and Working Script for
Polaroid Stories
A Model by Carrie Ann Quinn

(Author's Note: This is an abbreviated version of the original document.)

Notes on First Impressions (abstract/experiential)

- A labyrinth. Vertical labyrinth.

- Metamorphosis: A change of the form or nature of a thing or person into a completely different one, by natural or supernatural means.

- Street kids' souls and lives are defaced (graffiti) just as the environment is.

- In Hades. Need to get out. Edge of city . . . a "way stop."

Dramatic Questions

- Why do I like this play? It is poetic and musical and dangerous.

- Human values: Life is not precious; to live one must transform from one thing to another; anything is better than loneliness.

- Play makes me think about? Danger of wanting to be God-like/famous/rich. Limitations of humans versus gods. How we hurt children.

- How does play make me see the world in new way? That desire to be loved can appear in many forms.

- Metaphor that captures essence of play? Surrendering to the labyrinth. "A labyrinth is not a maze or a puzzle to be solved but a path of meaning to be experienced. Its path is circular and convoluted, but it has no dead ends. A labyrinth has one entrance—one way in and one way out" (Alex Patakos, HuffPost "Life & the Labyrinth of Meaning").

Defining the World of the Play

- Literal landscape versus emotional landscape—For both I see the labyrinth. A vertical labyrinth?

- Whose world is this? The gods' world: G and D and Persephone (less).

- 2015 Boston fictitious underground—red line? In the Fall?

- Historical, societal psychological issues in world? The downfall of mortal desire to be God-like, the "forgotten" throw-away fringe of society, child-abuse, drug-abuse, society's fringe/ugly. Inability to love or be loved. The economy of sex/love-trafficking of bodies. What are you worth $?

About the Characters

- Seeking to capture:

  - D—it's his Kingdom. He's the Host. (Wants to be G . . .) Abandoned/hurt by parents.

  - G—the old man. Pulling strings still? (D's father)

  - P—the Queen (used to be Semele, D's mother).

- Yes, there is an allusion to the father, son (savior), and Virgin Mary.

- Seeking to escape:

  - Eurydice—young, disillusioned, wants to be noticed/loved/independent.

  - Orpheus—musical, abusive.

  - Philomel—sings, no words, has been silenced.

  - Narcissus—a great liar, a raver (lives in fantasy world), self-destructive, cross-dress.

  - Echo—runaway girl, can't see herself, follows Narcissus.

  - Skinhead boy—speedracer, speedfreak, huffer, okie boy, loves a girl.

  - Skinhead girl/neon girl—punk, fast, reaching for the impossible, burning bright and out,

Layers of Thought

- This play is about_____

  - Longing for what we can't have.

  - The lure of self-destruction.

  - Futility of escape.

  - Metamorphosis: How people change (or don't).

  - "Say your name or disappear."

Spine/major dramatic question?

- Will the young humans find healing and their desires without destroying themselves? Will humans ever find the way out of the labyrinth?

- If no one remembers your name, did you ever exist?

Director Quinn's Concept and Working Script questionnaire offers an effective script analysis model for accessing the themes of a play. It is useful both in a professional setting and in the classroom (Figures 3.13–3.17).

Design Gallery: *Polaroid Stories*

FIGURE 3.13

Actors Christian Ruiz (Narcissus) and Cassidy Bane (Echo), *Polaroid Stories*, UMass Boston, Spring 2016. Playwright and Production Staff. Playwright: Naomi Izuka, Director: Carrie Ann Quinn, Dramaturge: Jen Elias, Scenic and Lighting Designer: Anthony Phelps, Costume Designer: Rafael Jaen, Sound Designer: Michael Katz, Makeup and Hair Design: Tori Moline, Props Master: Joe Sheehan, Stage Manager: Jaime Silva.

FIGURE 3.14

FIGURE 3.15

Sketch for Eurydice, *Polaroid Stories*, UMass Boston, Spring 2015. Photoshop technique: I used pre-existing garment images, copied and pasted them in separate layers, and painted them to look distressed. The same technique is used for **Figures 3.15**, **3.16**, and **3.17**. The next few chapters describe various painting techniques.

Sketch for Echo, *Polaroid Stories*, UMass Boston, Spring 2015.

FIGURE 3.16

Sketch for Narcissus, *Polaroid Stories*, UMass Boston, Spring 2015.

FIGURE 3.17

Sketch for G (Hades—Zeus), *Polaroid Stories*, UMass Boston, Spring 2015.

Citations and Sources

1   "Adobe Support." Adobe Support. Accessed August 17, 2015. https://helpx.adobe.com/support.html#/top_products.

2   Dictionary.com. Accessed August 17, 2016. http://dictionary.reference.com/browse/croquis.

3   "V63: ¾ View Female Croqui Fashion Figure Template." Designers Nexus. 2014. Accessed August 17, 2016. www.designersnexus.com/fashion-design-portfolio/v63-¾-view-female-croqui-fashion-figure-template/.

4   Jaen, Rafael. "Preparing Black and White Drawings." YouTube. February 02, 2013. Accessed August 17, 2016. www.youtube.com/watch?v=u98bUP3tNeU.

5   Jaen, Rafael. "Digital Costume Rendering—Prepping B & W Sketches on a Template." YouTube." YouTube. July 26, 2011. Accessed August 17, 2016. https://youtu.be/tR_cSyhjlKw.

6   Jaen, Rafael. "Digital Costume Rendering: Fixing Drawing Leakages with Photoshop." YouTube. July 26, 2011. Accessed August 17, 2016. www.youtube.com/watch?v=D8LNbXCELok.

7   Jaen, Rafael. "Digital Costume Rendering: Fixing Drawing Leakages with Photoshop." YouTube. July 26, 2011. Accessed August 17, 2016. www.youtube.com/watch?v=D8LNbXCELok.

CONTEXTUALIZE

VERB / CON.TEX.TU.AL.IZE

: TO THINK ABOUT OR PROVIDE INFORMATION ABOUT

THE SITUATION IN WHICH SOMETHING HAPPENS.

MERRIAM-WEBSTER DICTIONARY ONLINE[1]

CHAPTER 4

CONTEXTUALIZING THE CHARACTER

I have found that Photoshop is ideal to create costume renderings, because as a designer I can draw, paint, and do collages, as well as manipulate digital images, to express how I visualize each character in costume. Photoshop also allows me to give each costume piece or accessory item that is part of a costume design its own layer (labeled as such). In this chapter I continue to cover rendering techniques, and each tutorial has an accompanying video on my Rafael Jaen YouTube channel: www.youtube.com/user/JaenRafael/videos.

Photoshop Painting Basics

Photoshop Color Palettes: The Color Picker[2]

The Photoshop color palettes can be found within a small square on the lower part of the software left tool column. When you click on it, an interface window called Color Picker (Foreground Color) will come up. Though the palettes contain a finite set of colors, they offer "Color Libraries" options that are excellent for painting digital images. As you learn to use different modalities and special effects, you will discover many options that can add contrast, depth, and highlights to the color details in your sketches.

Steps

1. Open the image that you intend to paint, as well as reference images such as an actor's headshot for skin tone, a research board, or images representing the intended design color palette for the show.

2. Open Layers toolbar, Undo History toolbar, and Project Bin toolbar, which are found under the upper interface menu window (see Figures 4.1 and 4.2).

3. Start with the background.

4. Open your color palette located on the lower left side tool column by double-clicking on it.

5. Select [Only Web Colors]. This will allow you to open the file as a PDF, and email it to the director,

with trust that the colors will stay true to what you intended.

6. When you SAVE as a TIFF file, you can select RGB, which will allow you to go to the print shop knowing that the colors will be what you have chosen. Pantone swatches are also welcome.

7. Choose the color that best suits the tones of the play. In the case of the example, the director and I had discussed using lavender tones, as represented by the flowers in a painting he shared with me (see Figure 4.2).

8. Double-check that you are on the Background layer.

9. Select Paint Bucket.

10. Check that Mode is "Normal," and that the Opacity is 100% (you may decide to alter the Opacity after testing your chosen color).

11. "Dump" the chosen color into the background by clicking on the Paint Bucket icon.

12. You may now alter the color if it is too bright or dark to represent the play's tone.

13. To capture more of the play's atmosphere, you may choose to add texture or variety to the background by using a brush. In the example, I used the Brush tool, with a leaf-shaped tip, and white coloring (at a significantly lower Opacity), to add depth to the background (see Figure 4.3).

14. Always create a duplicate Silhouette layer named Hair & Makeup.

15. Sample the skin tone by pointing and clicking the Eyedropper tool on the selected actor's headshot. If you don't have a skin image to sample, you can click on the Foreground Color square (located at the bottom of your left column interface menu) and choose a palette that looks like the actor's skin tone.

FIGURE 4.1

Painting Basics, Steps 1—2. Actress Amy Ross' eye is featured in the background.

FIGURE 4.2

Painting Basics, Step 7.

FIGURE 4.3

Painting Basics, Step 13. You may choose to add texture or variety to the background by using a brush.

16. Zoom in by pressing [Command] > [+].

17. Double-check that you are on the right layer, which is the layer you intend to paint.

18. Switch to Paint Bucket tool.

19. Turn Opacity to 100%.

20. Fill the region, and check the color. You may decide to undo the dump, and lower Opacity if the color does not look right.

21. In the example, some skin shows through a see-through blouse. Here, while you have the skin color sampled, you can use a brush to create a suggestion of skin (see Figure 4.4), which will come through the fabric, and contrast with the bare skin regions.

22. Using the Eyedropper tool, sample the highlight of your actor's hair, and fill the drawing hair area. This layer is a base, and you can add shadows and highlights later.

23. Select Blouse layer, choose color, and fill the region. Lowering the Opacity will allow you to see through the blouse, onto the partially covered skin.

24. Select Skirt layer, choose color, and fill the region. If, like the example, the outfit is monochromatic but you need to contrast the transparency of another piece (i.e., the Blouse layer), raise the Opacity of the fill to 100%.

25. From here, continue to each layer to individually paint the character's costume and props.

26. Zoom out by pressing [Command] > [-].

27. View your basic painted sketch.

28. SAVE as . . . (Give it the character's name.)

Creating a Basic Sketch Template for a Specific Show[3]

The base (first) layer of a Photoshop rendering can be designed as a template for each specific show, with the show title and other repetitive information such as the director, the theatre company, the date, and the designer's name. Once created, we can make multiple copies to use with each costume sketch, so the format does not have to be recreated each time. Costume templates that use scenic elements in the base layer (or even an actual elevation) allow the designer to anchor the character in an environment that relates to the set design shapes and color palette, thus avoiding "the red costume, on the red couch, in front of the red wall" problem. Below I share some effective steps to creating sketch templates.

Steps

1. Select a JPEG of an image that you wish to use as a background; if you are grabbing something off the Internet, be aware that a larger image will work better than a small one.

2. If you are planning to use someone else's design work, for instance the set designer's sketch, be sure to secure that person's permission prior to creating the template.

3. Crop the image to the correct size by using the Marquee tool to select the region you intend to keep, then click [Image] > [Crop]. You can also use [Image] > [Edit] > [Free Transform] to make it the size that you prefer.

4. Choose the Text Box tool on the left interface, and add information about the show (for example: title, venue, director, date). Put your name and job title at the bottom, and always double-check the spelling of titles and other folk's names (see Figure 4.5).

FIGURE 4.4

Painting Basics, Step 21. You can use a brush to create a suggestion of skin.

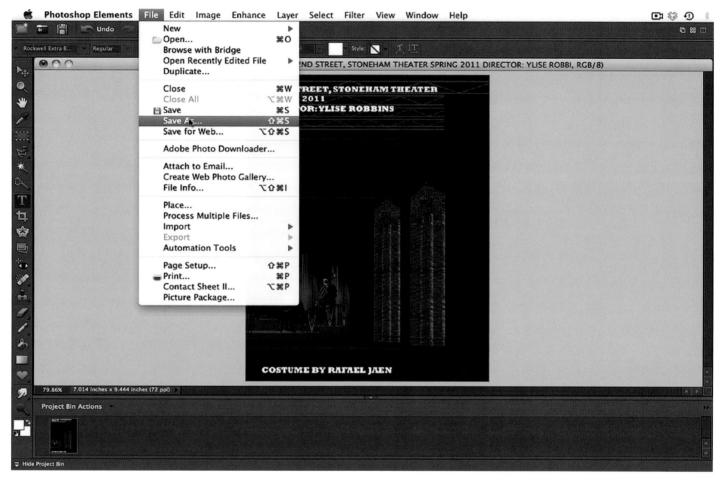

FIGURE 4.5

Creating a Template, Steps 4–5. Add information about the show (for example: title, venue, director, date).

5. Once the template is finished, go to [File] > [SAVE As] and choose JPEG in the drop-down menu, and then select the maximum #12 quality when prompted.

6. Check spelling and formatting once again.

7. SAVE once again, as a Photoshop image, so you will be able to edit the content (if needed) in the future.

Choosing Specific Photoshop Color Swatches for Costume Rendering[4]

Finding color swatches in Photoshop can be a daunting task; it is definitely not impossible, but adventurous instead. Depending on the software version (Elements, or the whole Creative Suite), there are some key things that designers need to locate.

Steps

1. Begin by selecting the Color Picker interface window. Depending on the number of options it gives you, move through these steps. You can also go directly to the upper banner choices under [Window] > [Color Swatches], or [Window] > [Color] (there may be more color options visible here); your choices will vary depending on your software number.

2. In Elements:

   a. Open Color Picker, select Only Web Colors.

   b. In the toolbar opened by the upper interface, there is a Photo Filter Colors option.

      i. I choose the Pantone option.

FIGURE 4.7

Finding Color Swatches, Step 2.b.ii.

ii. You can also change the view sometimes by clicking on the "More" option and selecting "Small Thumbnail" on the interface window (see Figures 4.6 and 4.7).

3. In the Creative Suite:

a. Open Color Picker. It should have more options, including Color Libraries, and the choice to use Only Web Colors.

b. Select Color Libraries in order to access more color swatches (see Figure 4.8).

c. Now choose one of the many options from the "Book" tab, for example, Pantone (see Figure 4.9).

d. One can also:

i. Go to [Window] > [Color].

ii. In the toolbar, go into Photo Filter Colors and select option (e.g., Pantone).

iii. In the same menu select Small Thumbnail.

Creating Fabric Yardage and Adding Prints[5]

The following demonstration samples a digital fabric swatch, and puts the pattern into a skirt. This technique becomes helpful when a director asks to see a different fabric color, pattern, or texture in a costume, after you have presented a finished sketch. With Photoshop you only have to make changes in the specific garment

FIGURE 4.8

Finding Color Swatches, Step 3.b.

CREATIVE SUITE COLOR PICKER

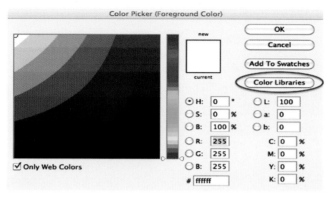

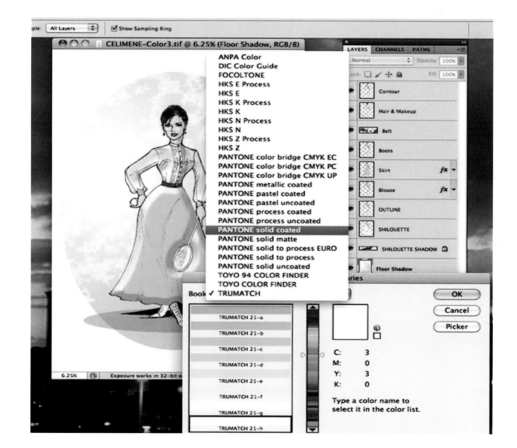

FIGURE 4.9

Finding Color Swatches, Step 3.c.

layer, e.g., the skirt, that belongs to the particular character, rather than drawing and painting a whole new sketch.

Steps

1. Open your color sketch, and fabric swatch file that you want to use.

2. Open the black & white character's silhouette that you SAVED within the first layers of your costume sketch.

3. Select the garment layer that you plan to edit—in this tutorial example, it is the blue skirt. Duplicate that layer twice. Name the first layer "Skirt Pattern," and the second layer "Cropped Fabric Skirt."

4. Hide the original "Blue Skirt" layer by clicking the Eye icon (on the left side) beside the layer's image.

5. Select the Skirt Pattern layer.

6. Select Brush tool, and set the color to white; make sure the tool is pretty large, in "Normal" mode, and has 100% Opacity.

7. Paint a white canvas on this new pattern layer. Use the Marquee tool to contain your white paint, and to create a clean, rectangular frame around the figure.

8. Hide other costume layers that are on top of the Skirt Pattern layer (see Figure 4.10).

9. Click on the Paint Bucket tool, and then switch from "Foreground" to "Pattern" in the tiny interface dialogue window to the right of the paint bucket symbol on the left side of the top row.

10. Normally a fabric swatch image should be sized to about 4"x4" to successfully drop into an 11x17 sketch (see Figure 4.11).

11. The image of the fabric swatch should have a resolution of 75 to 100 dpi so it reads well in the final sketch. You can check the image size by simply opening the JPEG with your computer's "Preview" function (instead of Photoshop) and by choosing "Tools" > "Adjust Size."

12. To resize your fabric swatch, go to [Image] > [Resize] > [Image Size] (see Figure 4.11).

13. SAVE this by going to [Edit] > [Define Pattern]. Your fabric swatch will now be SAVED in your Photoshop pattern archive (see Figure 4.12).

14. Select the newly SAVED fabric swatch from within the drop-down menu in your Photoshop patterns (see #9), and then click in your Paint Bucket tool to fill the rectangular white space that you just created. This will fill in the formerly white rectangular shape with the pattern creating "fabric yardage." Note: In the video example, there is a special effect still active from the skirt that had been on this layer. To undo this, click the special effects icon beside the layer's image, and remove the special effect (in this case, a bevel).

15. Open the Cropped Fabric Skirt layer, making sure that it is on top of the fabric yardage layer—you may need to click on it and drag it up to move it into place. Check the size accuracy of the fabric pattern in comparison to your character and the costume piece; the fabric pattern needs to relate to the human body, e.g., if a flower in a pattern is about three human fingers wide (in real life), the fabric yardage should correspond in size to the three fingers of the character's drawing in Photoshop.

16. Select the Magic Wand tool.

17. Click within the skirt, and then press delete to get rid of the blue.

18. Select Marquee tool, and click elsewhere to deselect the skirt (see Figure 4.13).

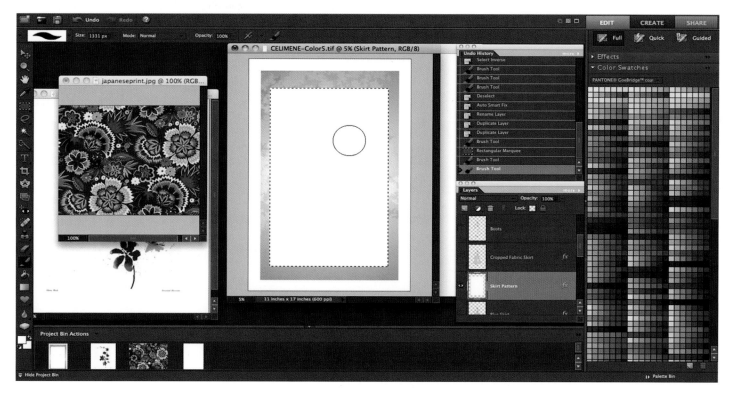

FIGURE 4.10

Fabric Yardage and Adding Prints, Steps 5–9.

Go to: Image > Resize > Image Size and change the meassurements
Resolution should be 75 minimum

FIGURE 4.11

Fabric Yardage and Adding Prints, Steps 11–12.

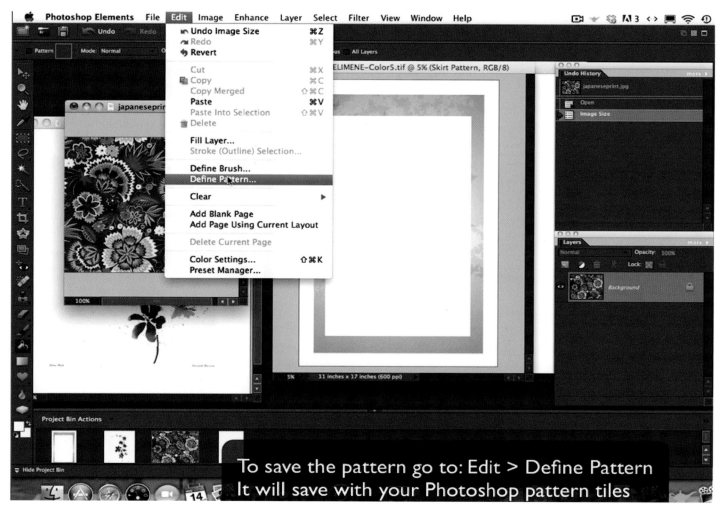

To save the pattern go to: Edit > Define Pattern
It will save with your Photoshop pattern tiles

FIGURE 4.12

Fabric Yardage and Adding Prints, Step 13.

Shape the new fabric by going to: Image > Transform > Perspective
OR Edit > Transform > Perspective

FIGURE 4.13

Fabric Yardage and Adding Prints, Step 18.

19. Switch to Skirt Pattern layer.

20. Reshape the fabric to an A-shape to match the movement of the skirt, by going to [Image] > [Transform] > [Perspective], OR [Edit] > [Transform] > [Perspective], and then click the boundaries and drag them to fit your needs. When finished, click the checkmark to finalize and SAVE your changes.

21. In addition, go to [Image] > [Transform] > [Skew]. Now you can change the angle further to match the angles of the skirt (one side has a steeper angle than the other). When finished, click the checkmark to finalize and SAVE your skewed pattern.

22. Switch to "Cropped Fabric Skirt" layer. Re-select Magic Wand tool, and highlight the skirt.

23. Go to [Select] > [Inverse]. Re-select large Brush tool, and paint white around the skirt to get rid of extra fabric.

24. Merge both the "Cropped Fabric Skirt" layer and "Skirt Pattern" layer. Do this by right clicking the upper layer, and selecting [Merge Down] to connect it with the one layer below. This step will merge just one layer below.

25. Select the newly combined layer.

26. Select Magic Wand tool.

27. Select the white area, and click delete to erase it.

28. To SAVE your work, press "Enter" or select the Marquee tool and click anywhere on the image.

29. Now you can add all of the layers that you had made invisible, with the exception of the "Blue Skirt" layer, by clicking on the eyes next to each layer.

30. Reopen the special effects (fx) lower tab on the right side column, in the new patterned skirt layer, and select [Bevel] to add depth and texture.

31. You can add more depth and texture by using the Color Burn modality in the upper row tabs.

32. Select the Eyedropper tool, and sample the darker, beveled cloth.

33. Select the Brush tool.

34. Make the brush smaller, sizing it by using the tiny interface window to the right of the brush icon on the upper row. Change mode from "Normal" to "Color Burn," and lighten the Opacity to about 10% or less. This will darken some of the existing areas to add depth and blend some of the bevel effect.

35. To lighten the color, select "Color Dodge" instead of "Burn." By using your brush in this modality, you will be able to add highlights and soften the bevel effect (see Figure 4.14).

Testimonial

DAVIS ROBINSON—PRODUCER, ACTOR, DIRECTOR, AND AUTHOR

I look to designers to help me understand a show and see what is physically needed to tell the story.

Bio

Davis Robinson teaches acting, directing, and courses in Theatre Styles, Comedy, Improvisation, Ensemble Devising, Physical Theatre, and Shakespeare. He has worked professionally as an actor and director around New England for over 20 years in film and television, and on stage. He often directs for the Shakespeare Theater at Monmouth, most recently *The Illusion*, *Our Town*, *Blithe Spirit*, and *Antony and Cleopatra*. He directed *Waiting for Godot* at the Theatre Project in Brunswick, and worked with the Columbian–American clown trio The Fabulous Problemas to develop their new show. In 2007, he was movement coach for the world premiere of Leslie Epstein's *King of the Jews* in Boston. Recent shows for

FIGURE 4.14

Fabric Yardage and Adding Prints, Steps 28–34.

Bowdoin include *Light/Dark*, *End of Summer*, *A Little Night Music*, and *The Cripple of Inishmaan*. He trained in Paris with Jacques LeCoq, and is particularly interested in movement-based theatre, forgotten American plays, and the creation of original productions adapted from films, novels, and current events.

For several years he worked closely at Emerson College with renowned voice teacher Kristin Linklater. He is also founder and artistic director of the award-winning Beau Jest Moving Theater with whom he acts, writes, directs, and tours nationwide, including runs off-Broadway and appearances at Lincoln Center and the Piccolo Spoleto Festival in Charleston, SC. Beau Jest recently staged three Tennessee Williams world-premieres for the Provincetown Tennessee Williams Festival, and toured the rarely seen original one-act *Ten Blocks on the Camino Real*. They are currently touring an original comic-noir fantasy, *Apt 4D*. In June 2015, Professor Robinson published a new book with Palgrave Macmillan on developing original material called *A Practical Guide to Ensemble Devising*. His book *The Physical Comedy Handbook* was published by Heinemann in 1999. His current research interests include Tennessee Williams, objects in action, and new methods for combining text and physicality in the devising process. Davis studied movement and improvisation for many years with Tony Montanaro at the Celebration Barn Theater, where he teaches devising every summer.

Interview

Rafael: What are your beliefs (or approach) in regard to collaborating with designers?

Davis: I like designers who can read my mind. I don't think like a designer and I don't have very clear images of what a show might look like until after I talk to the designers about a show and do some brainstorming with them. The initial discussions usually lead to some research images or sketches that begin to zero in on creating something specific. I do know what I love when I see it. I look to designers to help me understand a show and see what is physically needed to tell the story. Once I find designers who are skilled at interpreting a text or other source material, designers who like to collaborate on an intuitive level initially and are able to put inspired ideas into practice and use input from everyone involved in the show, I like to hang onto that team and work with them on future shows. It is much easier to reference previous projects when you have developed a body of work together.

Rafael: Is there a "mantra" or core belief that you subscribe to when directing a production?

Davis: Whenever I direct a show, my core belief is to be true to the source material. I usually begin by reading biographies, letters, and background information on the show to see what questions drove the author to write the play. I also always consider why it is important to do this play now, and look at how it speaks to a contemporary audience. Designers are an early and important part of that research phase and are key to developing the approach to the play long before actors are cast and rehearsals begin. I need to know what world we are playing in, and what the set/sound/costume options will be for the actors to work with. Designers help determine what expressive tools will be used to tell the story. I rely on designers to see and solve problems before rehearsals begin, and to be part of the rehearsal process early on so that they can respond to any new discoveries made by the cast while there is still time to make changes. They may have done the show before, or come to the table with inspired ideas, but every show involves a certain degree of discovery that can't be anticipated and may require some quick adjustments or bold changes made at the last minute. With good communication, trust, and respect, this way of working can turn a good show into a great show.

Rafael: How would you describe your collaborative approach when working with a designer for the first time?

Davis: When I am hired by a theatre to work with a designer for the first time, I like to have a phone conversation or meeting to talk in general about how they like to work, about my working methods, and then to speak about the show's budget, needs, timelines, and other practical considerations. The next conversations are the most important—zeroing in on a vision for the show, and communicating with all of the designers so that the world of the play is unified. If this is being done long distance (as is often the case these days), drawings, research materials, and final renderings may all be done through Google docs, shared Dropbox folders, or other means so that one arm knows what the other is doing. It's an odd way to collaborate, but if you work with people who are good at their jobs, it's not unusual for the director, the cast, the producers, and the design team to meet each other for the first time during tech week.

Design Gallery: *The Remarkable Rooming House of Madame LeMonde*

The world premiere production of a savage comedy by Williams, written late in his life. Tea-time turns into torment, and desperation into absurd laughter. From Boston's acclaimed Beau Jest Moving Theatre, celebrating its 25th Anniversary this year. Set in a boarding house in London, a mysteriously paralyzed man named Mint moves around his attic by swinging from hooks as he prepares for tea with an old friend . . . . A dark, disturbing tale with a sinister sense of humor, originally written to shock—as part of an evening of Grand Guignol that was never produced. This memorable play is a must-see for anyone interested in the great playwright's experimental work.[6]

FIGURE 4.15

Actors Lisa Tucker as Madame LeMonde, Nick Ronan as Son, Jordan Harrison as Mint, and Larry Coen as Hall. *The Remarkable Rooming House of Madame LeMonde*, by Tennessee Williams, Directed by Davis Robinson, Produced by Beau Jest Moving Theatre, Costume Design by Rafael Jaen, Set Design by Deb Puhl and David Howe, Lighting Design by Colin Deick and Megan Tracy, Sound Design by Rew Tippen, Graphic Design by Judy Gailen, Photography by Bill O'Connell.

Mme. Le Monde

FIGURE 4.16

Sketch for Madame LeMonde. Beau Jest 2009. I used Photoshop patterns and the Disolve modaltiy.

FIGURE 4.17

Sketch for Mint. Beau Jest 2009.

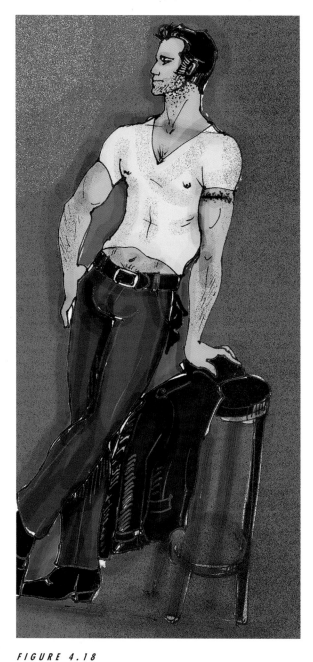

FIGURE 4.18

Sketch for the Son. Beau Jest 2009. I also used the Dodge and Burn modalities.

FIGURE 4.19

Sketch for Hall. Beau Jest 2009.

Citations and Sources

1   "Contextualize / Definition by Merriam Webster."
    Merriam-Webster. Accessed August 29, 2016.
    www.merriam-webster.com/dictionary/
    contextualize.

2   Jaen, Rafael. "Photoshop Painting Basics Part
    1." YouTube. 2013. Accessed August 29, 2016.
    www.youtube.com/watch?v=YCtofvCszVI. Video:
    Photoshop Painting Basics Part 1.

3   Jaen, Rafael. "Creating a Basic Sketch Template."
    YouTube. 2011. Accessed August 29, 2016.
    www.youtube.com/watch?v=6T_d1N50c6g. Video:
    Creating a Basic Sketch Template.

4   Jaen, Rafael. "Photoshop Color Swatches
    for Costume Rendering." YouTube. 2015.
    Accessed August 29, 2016. www.youtube.com/
    watch?v=bPkhwQXTshQ. Video: Finding Photoshop
    Color Swatches for Costume Rendering.

5   Jaen, Rafael. "Creating Fabric Yardage and Adding
    Prints." YouTube. 2014. Accessed August 29, 2016.
    www.youtube.com/watch?v=KV-4hBWQQkM. Video:
    Creating Fabric Yardage and Adding Prints.

6   "Provincetown Tennessee Williams Theater
    Festival—Madame LeMonde." Accessed September
    01, 2016. http://twptown.org/madame-lemonde.

PRELIMINARY | PRE.LIM.I.NARY

NOUN

: SOMETHING THAT COMES FIRST IN ORDER TO PREPARE FOR

OR INTRODUCE THE MAIN PART OF SOMETHING ELSE

MERRIAM-WEBSTER DICTIONARY ONLINE[1]

CHAPTER 5

COSTUMING THE CHARACTER: THE PRELIMINARY SKETCHES

The methods in the following pages allow designers to draw and paint each costume article, adding specific fabric details (such as fabric patterns), in separate Photoshop layers. The approach facilitates making specific apparel changes and updates due to a design, directorial, or rehearsal note. New Photoshop layer garments can be added to the same sketch to allow the designer to explore different colors and patterns, and old layers can easily become "invisible." Each tutorial has a video companion on my YouTube channel: www.youtube.com/user/JaenRafael/videos.

Creating Multi-Layered Costume Renderings in Photoshop[2]

Steps

1. Open B & W Silhouette (also know as the B & W Sketch).

2. Open Undo History toolbar by clicking [Window] > [Undo History].

3. Open Layers toolbar by clicking [Windows] > [Layers].

4. Zoom in with [Command] > [+].

5. While working with the layers, remember that you can make particular layers visible or invisible by clicking the Eye icon, to the left of each layer, on the Layer toolbar.

6. Make the background invisible by clicking the Eye icon.

7. Look for leakages (Chapter 3), and fix them with colors from your palette. Zoom in and out as necessary, and use the Undo History toolbar to erase any accidents (see Figure 5.1).

8. Do not worry about damaging the drawing with thick lines. It is better to have to go back later to edit back in the thin lines than it is to find leakages later on in the process.

FIGURE 5.1

Look for leakages, and fix them with colors from your "Color Picker" palette.

FIGURE 5.2

To insert a pattern through a difficult, divided section of the drawing (i.e., the racket in the example picture), draw thin white lines through the boundaries to create purposeful—and invisible—leakages.

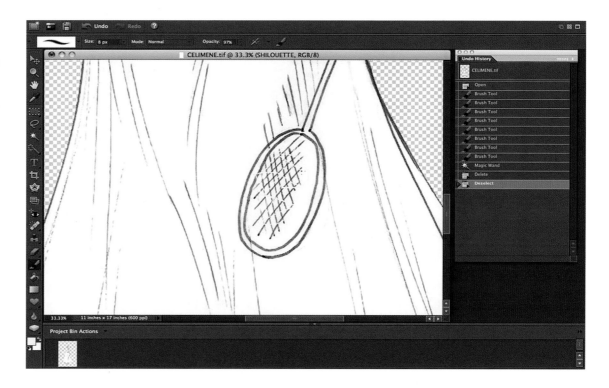

9. While editing leakages, look for white background sections that may still connect your character's limbs, accessories, belongings, etc.

10. If you're planning to insert a pattern through a difficult, divided section of the drawing (i.e., the racket in the example picture), draw thin white lines through the boundaries to create purposeful—and invisible—leakages (see Figure 5.2).

11. Zoom out to see the full image by clicking [Command] > [-].

12. Duplicate the B & W Sketch/Silhouette image, and name it "Outline." You can do this by either right clicking on the image layer's picture (on the Layer toolbar), or by using the upper interface: [Layer] > [Duplicate].

13. Make the B & W Sketch/Silhouette layer invisible. You could SAVE a copy of it as a separate document if you anticipate future changes or if you need to go back and edit it from the start. The original B & W Silhouette Sketch can also be useful to many other aspects of design presentation, e.g., when looking at the placement of seams or darts in a build costume, the line drawing can help the draper/cutter discern your intended placement.

14. Select Magic Wand and delete the white section in the Outline layer. Holding the [Shift] key while clicking will allow you to select multiple sections to delete at once.

15. When finished, press "Enter" to SAVE this Outline layer. Sometimes the Magic Wand freezes; if this happens with your Photoshop version, select the Marquee tool and click anywhere else in the image to get out of Magic Wand and SAVE the Outline layer.

16. To darken the image slightly, go to the Photoshop top bar (upper row) and click: [Enhance] > [Adjust Lighting] > [Levels . . .] (see Figure 5.3).

17. Count the number of costume pieces that you have in your sketch and make duplicates of the Outline layer, e.g., if you have five pieces copy the layer five times. To duplicate it, double-click on the layer (located in the lower right column window) and choose "Duplicate" when the tiny dialogue interface window opens. You will need one Photoshop layer for each costume piece (or clothing piece) so you

can edit them separately. In my example, I needed five outline layers for the hair/skin/makeup, blouse, skirt, belt, and shoes (see Figure 5.4).

18. After duplicating the edited B & W Silhouette that we are now calling the Outline layer, name each new layer to correspond with its respective costume piece.

19. You are now able to work on each costume piece/ section separately!

Inserting and Manipulating Costume Pieces or Elements[3]

Fabric patterns can present a challenge. Photoshop has tools that will allow the designer to introduce an impression of a fabric or, as illustrated in the previous chapter, an actual replica of a fabric print.

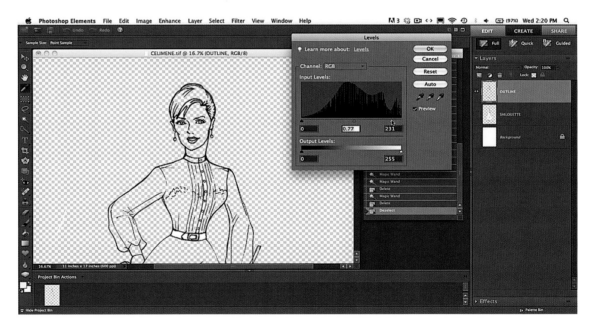

FIGURE 5.3

To darken the image, open the upper interface and click: [Enhance] > [Adjust Lighting] > [Levels...].

FIGURE 5.4

You will need one layer for each costume piece.

Steps

1. Open B & W Silhouette (Outline) Sketch and other needed images, such as a fabric pattern or an actual garment.

2. Duplicate B & W Silhouette (Outline) layer (see Figure 5.5).

3. Using the Lasso tool (found in the left tool column), outline the desired fabric pattern or costume piece. After the flickering dotted line appears, copy the image by going to the uppermost menu and choosing Edit > Copy, or by clicking [Command] + [c] (see Figure 5.6).

4. Next, paste the copied fabric pattern (or copied costume piece) onto the duplicated B & W Outline layer.

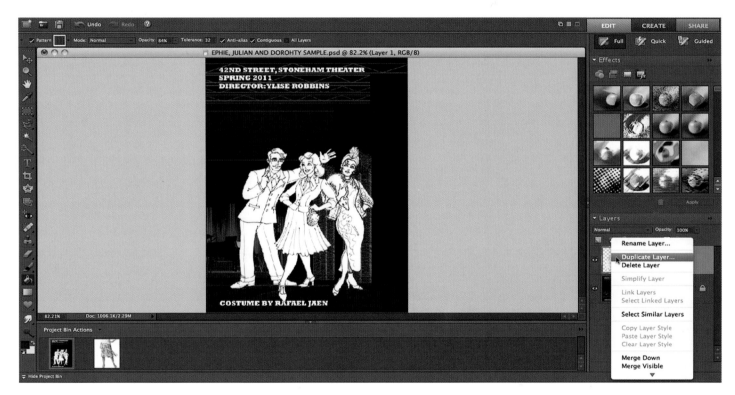

FIGURE 5.5

After opening the Black & White Silhouette Sketch, duplicate the layer.

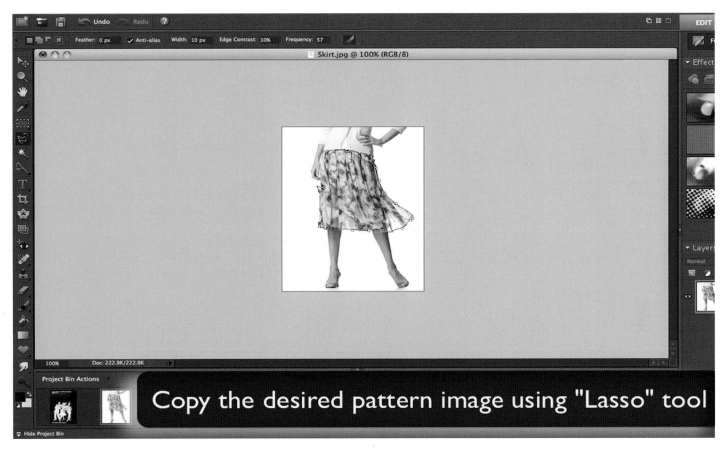

FIGURE 5.6

Use the Lasso tool to (outline) grab and copy patterns and images.

5. You can check the copied pattern layer placement by closing the Eye button, found on the lower right interface, on the left side of the new pattern's layer. This function allows you to see what's under the new layer (Figure 5.7).

6. Next, go to: [Image] > [Transform] > [Free Transform] and resize it or move it.

7. Always plan to resize the (pasted) image by clicking [Command] + [t], and after a rectangle framing the image appears, move its corners up/down or left/right till you obtain the desired size. And press "Enter" to SAVE it (or press "SAVE" if a dialogue window appears). Next, click on the image and drag it till it is in the proper costume piece area, and press "Enter" again to SAVE it.

8. Use the Erase tool in the left side tool column to clean up around the image if you see any shadows or marks. Sometimes they are carried over when pasting new images.

9. Click on the B & W Silhouette (Outline) layer, and drag it to the top.

10. Select Magic Wand.

11. Select the (white) area of the B & W Silhouette Outline layer that you want to delete, so you can see the new image.

12. The new costume piece (on the Photoshop under-layer) is now visible!

13. Click "Enter" to SAVE, or switch to the Marquee tool and click anywhere on the screen to SAVE.

Inserting a Pre-Existing or a Previously Saved Pattern

The Photoshop software comes with pre-existing patterns; below are the steps used to access them.

Steps

1. Click on the Paint tool on the left column and then locate it in the left upper row.

2. Open the arrow in the tiny dialogue window next to the paint icon, and switch from "Foreground" to "Pattern."

3. Choose a specific Photoshop pattern from the drop-down menu by clicking on it.

4. Move Paint tool and click on the desired layer of the sketch to dump the Photoshop pattern inside it.

5. Remember to SAVE your file before editing further.

Resizing Patterns in Photoshop[4]

Steps

1. Open the sketch you intend to paint, and the chosen Photoshop pattern.

2. Go to the B & W Silhouette Sketch. Make sure the Photoshop layer where you intend to use the fabric pattern is visible by making sure that the Eye icon to the left of it is visible.

3. Check that all the upper row Photoshop interface tools are at the right settings (Mode: Normal and Opacity: 100%).

4. Dump the fabric pattern into the Photoshop layer using Paint Bucket.

5. To resize, go to [Image] > [Transform] > [Free Transform] or press [Command] + [t]. Scale the Photoshop pattern down by dragging the corner downwards (see Figure 5.9).

6. Click "Enter" or the checkmark in the dialogue window to SAVE it (see Figure 5.8).

7. Go to [Image] > [Crop] in order to remove excess space.

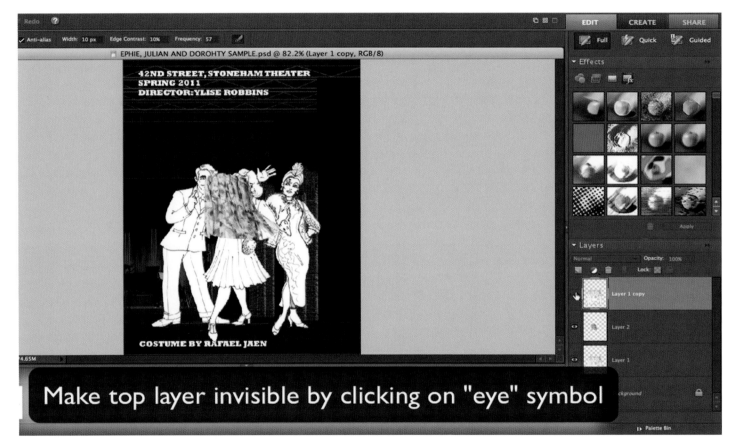

Make top layer invisible by clicking on "eye" symbol

FIGURE 5.7

The Eye button (on the lower right interface tool column) makes Photoshop layers visible and invisible.

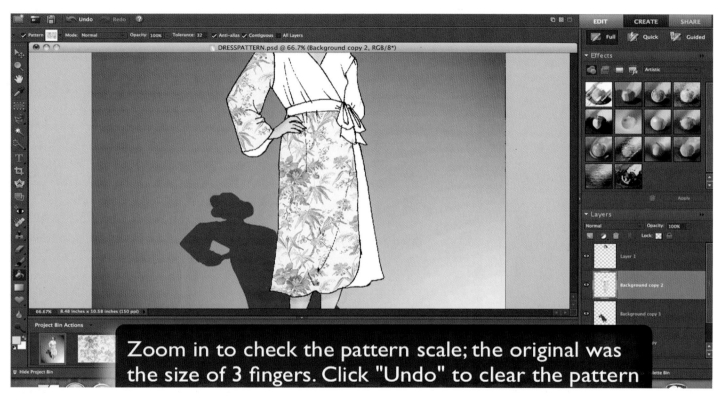

Zoom in to check the pattern scale; the original was the size of 3 fingers. Click "Undo" to clear the pattern

FIGURE 5.8

To resize the Photoshop pattern, go to [Image] > [Transform] > [Free Transform].

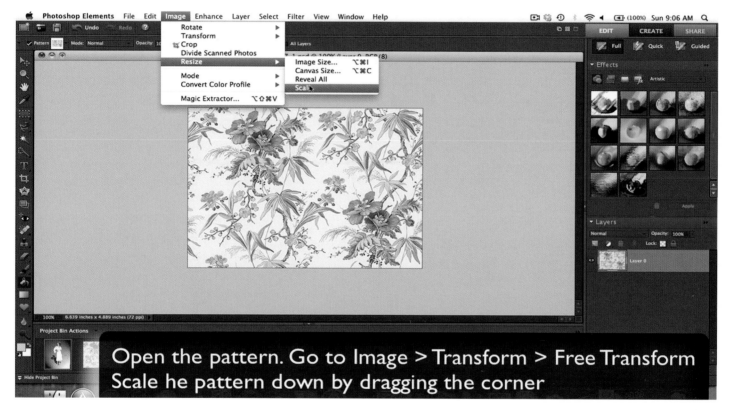

Open the pattern. Go to Image > Transform > Free Transform
Scale he pattern down by dragging the corner

FIGURE 5.9

Click the checkmark to save the updated Photoshop pattern.

8. Next, go to [Edit] > [Define Pattern] to SAVE the new (fixed pattern) size.

9. Fill the sketch with the newly SAVED re-sized Photoshop pattern (see Figure 5.10).

10. Add shadows and highlights with the Brush tool.

11. Choose Web Colors and Burn mode (at 50% or less).

12. To avoid painting beyond the desired area e.g., outside the robe, use the Magic Wand on the layer and then go to [Select] > [Inverse] (Figure 5.11).

13. The sketch's shape is now isolated, and can be painted with shadows and highlights without painting any of the surrounding areas. Use the Burn mode to add fabric shadows, and the Brush Tool in Normal mode, with low Opacity to add depth (see Figure 5.12).

14. To add text, click on the "T" tool (left tool column). The upper tool row will change to show various text modalities. Choose the font style, color, and size from this upper row menu.

Adding Layers such as Facial Details, Skin Tones, and Accessories[5]

Designers can use the Lasso tool as a time-saving device to add facial details, specific accessories, and the like to costume renderings.

Steps

(Adding Layers such as Facial Details)

1. Open B & W Silhouette and other needed images.

2. Using the Lasso tool (found in the left tool column interface), outline and then copy the face (see Figure 5.13).

3. Paste the face into the B & W Silhouette Sketch layer.

4. Click on the face layer and drag it to the top. Make sure that it is visible by clicking the Eye button (found on the right tool interface column, to the left of the layer).

5. Go to: [Image] > [Transform] > [Free Transform].

6. Drag, resize, pivot, double-check positioning, and move till the face and original image fit properly into the B & W Silhouette Sketch on the screen. When finished, click "Enter" or click on the checkmark in the dialogue window to SAVE it (see Figure 5.14).

7. Bring the B & W Silhouette Sketch image back to the top layer.

8. Zoom in by clicking: [Command] > [+].

9. Select the Erase tool, making sure to match its color to the background color. You can do this by clicking on the background layer with the Eyedropper tool while the Eraser tool is open. If a "hidden layer" warning pops up, it means that you are on the wrong layer (see Figure 5.15).

10. Select the Eyedropper to sample skin color(s) from the face, and then switch to the Paint Bucket to fill the appropriate skin layers, such as hands, etc.

11. Fix gap between face and the B & W Silhouette Sketch using the sampled skin tones and the Brush tool.

12. SAVE the sketch for further editing by clicking "Enter" or the checkmark in the dialogue window.

Painting Assembly Line Sketches[6]

When painting sketches traditionally, some designers may lay out as many as six renderings next to each other. This method allows them to paint in an assembly line; for example, they can fill in all the dark tones, skin tones, etc. to accelerate the process. They can do the same in Photoshop.

The scale is now correct!

FIGURE 5.10

Fill the sketch with the resized Photoshop pattern.

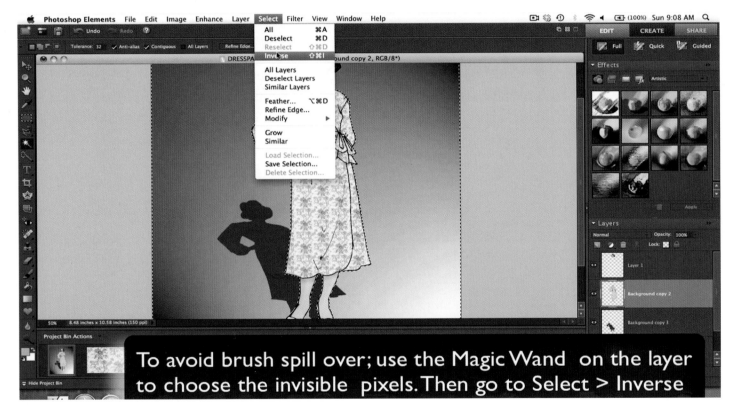

To avoid brush spill over; use the Magic Wand on the layer to choose the invisible pixels. Then go to Select > Inverse

FIGURE 5.11

To avoid painting beyond the desired area use the Magic Wand on the layer and then go to [Select] > [Inverse].

FIGURE 5.12

Use the Burn mode to add fabric shadows, and the Brush Tool in Normal mode, with low Opacity to add depth.

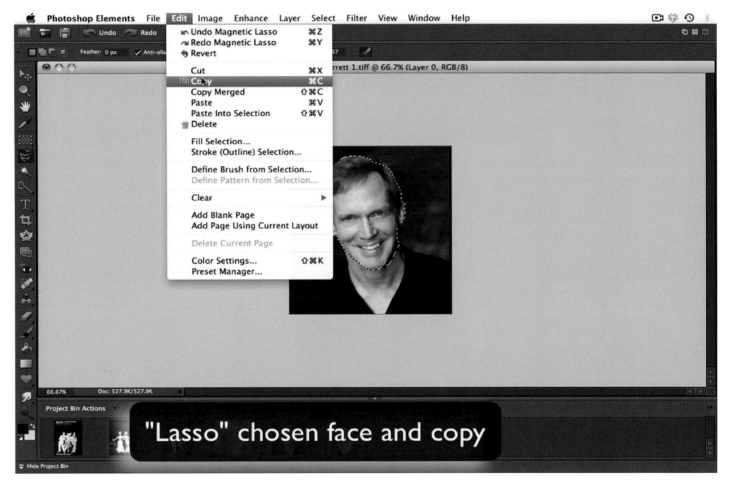

FIGURE 5.13

Using the Lasso tool (found in the left interface), outline then copy the face. Model: Actor Russell Garrett (as Julian Marsh) for the show *42nd Street*, at Stoneham Theatre in MA, May 5–29, 2011. The artistic support team included Ilyse Robbins (directing and choreography), Kathryn Kawecki (scenic design), Rafael Jaen (costume design), Jeff Adelberg (lighting design), Sarah Rozen (props), and pianist Jim Rice (musical director).

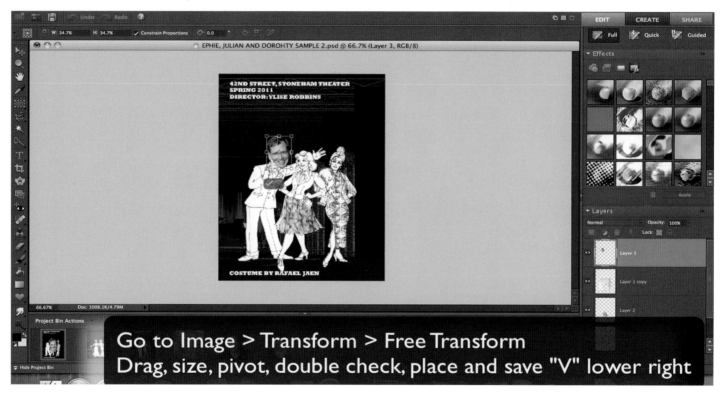

Go to Image > Transform > Free Transform
Drag, size, pivot, double check, place and save "V" lower right

FIGURE 5.14

Drag, resize, pivot, and double-check the fit of the face image.

FIGURE 5.15

The Erase tool can match the background color to make white areas disappear.

Steps

1. Open two to four sketches (depending on how many fit on your screen).

2. Offset them—click on the green button (upper left side).

3. Align sketches in order to paint the areas that repeat—such as skin tones, accessories, etc. Base the color tones on your palette (see Figure 5.16).

4. Make sure to be on the correct Photoshop layer (i.e., the layer with figures, instead of the background layer).

5. Using the Paint Bucket, fill all areas that have similar colors (such as faces, arms, legs, hands, etc.).

6. The idea is to make the more repetitive aspects of the painting process in Photoshop move quickly and smoothly, like an assembly line, which should SAVE time (see Figures 5.17 and 5.18).

7. Prepare for the next set of areas to be painted.

8. Use the Magic Wand tool to remove the unneeded background, as these areas may become more visible (and in the way) when you proceed to the painting stages.

Testimonial 1

ILYSE ROBBINS—ACTOR, CHOREOGRAPHER, AND DIRECTOR

Give and take—that's the most important thing.

Bio

Ilyse Robbins is a director, choreographer, actress, and teacher in the New England area. Ilyse holds a BS in Communication/Theatre from Northwestern University, certification in theatre from the British American Drama Academy, and an Ed.M. from Harvard University. Ilyse teaches critical thinking, story theatre, and dance history at Wheelock College and creative drama education for Brandeis University. Ilyse is on the staff of Mohr Collaborative as a presentation coach. Direction/choreography/performance credits include: Stoneham Theatre, Lyric Stage Company of Boston, New Repertory Theatre, Hanover Theatre, Underground Railway Theatre, Fiddlehead Theatre, Overture Productions, Jewish Theater of New England, American Stage Festival, Boston Theatre Works, Wheelock Family Theatre, Museum of Science, Publick Theatre, Boston Women on Top Festival, Boston Theater Marathon, Liberty Mutual, and Fidelity. Ilyse received the 2014 Elliot Norton Award for Best Direction for her production of *Thoroughly Modern Millie* and is the recipient of four Independent Reviewer of New England (IRNE) awards, most recently for her choreography for *42nd Street* (both at Stoneham Theatre).

Interview

Rafael: What are your beliefs (or approach) in regard to collaborating with designers?

Ilyse: What makes a good collaboration is a team of artists with patience, talent, and skill. Give and take—that's the most important thing. The designers and the director/choreographer must be willing to listen to each other, brainstorm together, dream big together, and each make allowances for the other. I love a costume designer who takes movement and footwear into consideration and a set person who takes floors and stairs into consideration. I love a designer who has a vision and can share and exchange with the director/choreographer. My favorite designers delve into the psyche of the character, the meat of the story, and the themes of the play.

FIGURE 5.16

Align sketches in order to paint the areas that repeat, such as skin tones, accessories, etc.

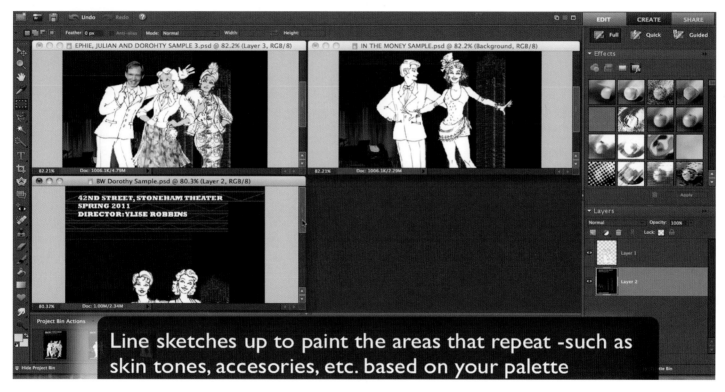

Line sketches up to paint the areas that repeat -such as skin tones, accesories, etc. based on your palette

FIGURE 5.17

The idea is to make the more repetitive aspects of the painting process in Photoshop move quickly and smoothly.

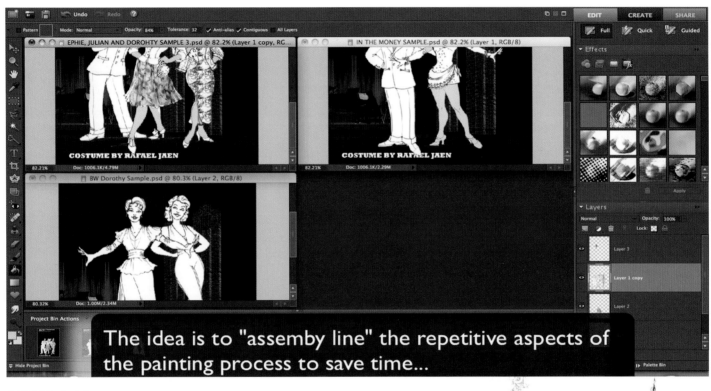

FIGURE 5.18

Painting Assembly Line Sketches, Steps 5–6.

Rafael: Is there a "mantra" or core belief that you subscribe to when directing a production?

Ilyse: Tell the story. Always say "yes" first. Find the joy in what you are doing, even when it is serious, and never ever forget that we call this a "play."

Design Gallery: *Marry Me a Little*

[An] updated take on Sondheim's charming musical revue—and on modern-day marriage. *Marry Me A Little* weaves songs from Sondheim's vault of unproduced shows and cutouts from his known musicals. Through bittersweet soliloquies and song, lonely New York singles fantasize romantic adventures, join in emotional conflict, and question the commitment of marriage—all the while never actually meeting.[7] (See Figures 5.19–5.21.)

FIGURE 5.19

New Repertory Theatre, *Marry Me a Little*. Artistic Team: Ilyse Robbins, Director/Choreographer; David McGrory, Music Director; Erik Diaz, Set Designer; Rafael Jaen, Costume Designer; Christopher Ostrom, Lighting Designer; David Reiffel, Sound Designer; Joe Stalone, Props Designer; Meghan Fisher, Production Stage Manager. Winter 2013.

New Repertory Theater
Directed By: Ilyse Robbins
Costumes: Rafael Jaen

C.D. 4434
COSTUME DESIGNER
SIGNATURE

Man 1: The Courier, Phil

New Repertory Theater
Directed By: Ilyse Robbins
Costumes: Rafael Jaen

C.D. 4434
COSTUME DESIGNER
SIGNATURE

Woman 1: Music Student, Erica

FIGURE 5.20

Photoshop sketch for Man 1. I used multiple layers for each garment and I used the Lasso tool to grab specific details such as the bicycle.

FIGURE 5.21

Photoshop sketch for Woman 1. I used multiple layers for each garment, and I used the Lasso tool to grab specific details such as the violin.

Testimonial 2

DANNY GIDRON—DIRECTOR

The question we need to pose for ourselves is 'what can I do *for* this play?' rather than 'what can I do *to* this play?'

Bio

Daniel Gidron was born in Israel, earned Fulbright and Wien Scholarships, and received his MFA from Brandeis University. Daniel has taught at Tel Aviv University, Hebrew University of Jerusalem, and Brandeis. He currently teaches at UMass Boston. In Israel he has directed for Habimah National Theatre, Haifa Municipal Theatre, Arab Theatre in Israel (*Accidental Death of an Anarchist*), and Beersheva Municipal Theatre (*Beauty Queen of Leenane*). Directing credits in the USA include Peterborough Players, Lyric Stage Company of Boston, Gloucester Stage, Merrimack Repertory, Opera Boston, New Repertory Theatre, and Nora Theatre Company, where he served as Associate Director. Recent productions include *Golda's Balcony*, *Full Gallop*, *Master Class* (Shakespeare and Company), *Groundswell, Or, The Chosen* (Lyric Stage), *Double Bill of Zanetto* and *Il Segreto di Susanna* (Odyssey Opera), *Hysteria*, *Photograph 51*, *The How and the Why*, *Absurd Person Singular*, and *Insignificance* (Nora). His production of *Arabian Nights* (a co-production of Nora and Underground Railway Theater) won the 2012 Independent Reviewers of New England (IRNE) award for Best Direction and is being revived for the fifth time.

Interview

Rafael: What are your beliefs (or approach) in regard to collaborating with designers?

Danny: I try to talk about the play and my take on it, leaving enough room for the designers to contribute to the process. I'm always looking to be surprised and inspired by the designers. I attempt to create a working relationship which allows the designer to "go to town" and experiment.

Rafael: Is there a "mantra" or core belief that you subscribe to when directing a production?

Danny: I believe that directors and designers are at the service of the playwright, whether (s)he is alive or dead. We are there to serve the play and to clarify, to the best of our abilities, the world of the play to our modern audiences. Creating the world of the play should be our objective. The question we need to pose for ourselves is "what can I do *for* this play?" rather than "what can I do *to* this play?"

Rafael: How would you describe your collaborative approach when working with designers for the first time?

Danny: I usually talk to the designer and try to sense what makes him (her) tick. It's a kind of "courtship" when you work with a designer for the first time. You need to go on a few dates before you become truly acquainted with each other. After that, the collaborative process is easier.

Design Gallery: *Twelfth Night*

[*Twelfth Night*] is the story of Viola who assumes the identity of a man 'Cesario' and is hired by Duke Orsino of Illyria. Duke Orsino is in love with Lady Olivia, who has sworn off marrying for seven years. The Duke asks 'Cesario' to assist him in wooing Lady Olivia. The situation gets complicated when Olivia falls in love with the disguised Viola, who herself begins to have feelings for her employer Duke Orsino. It deals with love and cross-dressing. Gender questions abound, and there are a lot of mistaken identities, music, license, and puritanism.[8] (See Figures 5.22–5.26.)

FIGURE 5.22

Twelfth Night. Playwright: William Shakespeare, Director: Daniel Gidron, Scenic and Lighting Designer: Anthony Phelps, Costume and Hair/Makeup Designer: Rafael Jaen, Sound Designer: Vanessa Charles, Props Master: Shannon Doane, Stage Manager: Walker Allison. UMass Boston, Theatre Arts. Spring 2014.

FIGURE 5.23

Photoshop sketch for the twins Viola and Sebastian. I took photos of actual fabric patterns and resized them.

FIGURE 5.24

Photoshop sketch for Maria and Fabiana.

FIGURE 5.25

Photoshop sketch for the Fool.

FIGURE 5.26

Photoshop sketch for the Priest and Malvolio.

Citations and Sources

1   Merriam-Webster. Accessed August 29, 2016. www.merriam-webster.com/dictionary/preliminary.

2   Jaen, Rafael. "Creating Multiple-Layered Costume Renderings in Photoshop." YouTube. 2013. Accessed August 30, 2016. www.youtube.com/watch?v=r62U4NHhGgM.

3   Jaen, Rafael. "Digital Costume Rendering—Inserting Fabric Patterns." YouTube. 2011. Accessed August 30, 2016. www.youtube.com/watch?v=VoJ_Wx7zQJE.

4   Jaen, Rafael. "Digital Costume Rendering: Re-sizing Patterns in Photoshop." YouTube. 2011. Accessed August 30, 2016. www.youtube.com/watch?v=BXs4ICrRmgY.

5   Jaen, Rafael. "Digital Costume Rendering—Adding Layers such as Faces." YouTube. 2011.

Accessed August 30, 2016. www.youtube.com/watch?v=llHthxNwycE.

6   Jaen, Rafael. "Digital Costume Rendering—Painting Assembly Line Sketches." YouTube. 2011. Accessed August 30, 2016. www.youtube.com/watch?v=xGI8Ec2P-oI.

7   "Marry Me a Little—New Repertory Theatre." New Repertory Theatre. Accessed August 30, 2016. www.newrep.org/productions/marry-me-a-little/.

8   Posted: Tuesday, April 15, 2014 3:49 p.m. "UMass Boston's Spring Production of 'Twelfth Night' Underway." Accessed September 01, 2016. http://m.umassmedia.com/mobile/art_lifestyle/umass-boston-s-spring-production-of-twelfth-night-underway/article_1c797014-c4d7-11e3-b012-001a4bcf6878.html.

FINISHED / FIN.ISHED

ADJECTIVE

: NOT REQUIRING MORE WORK : ENTIRELY DONE OR COMPLETED.

MERRIAM-WEBSTER DICTIONARY ONLINE[1]

CHAPTER 6

COSTUMING THE CHARACTER: THE FINISHED SKETCH

More Photoshop Painting Techniques

Photoshop is comparable to various painting media. For example, darker layers can be underneath semi-transparent ones, in the same way in which pure (lightly dissolved) pigments are laid down first when painting in watercolor. Photoshop painting can be versatile, ranging from a "transparent" watercolor look, to a "flat" tempera look, or to a "brilliant" acrylic look. The software tools replace the pigments, (liquid) binders, fixatives, additives, and solvents used in traditional painting techniques. Additionally, when using the software, renderings can seem translucent or luminous by using different levels of transparency and tool modalities.

The next pages reference digital costume sketches developed in previous chapters and demonstrate various techniques and tools featured in the accompanying video tutorials on my Rafael Jaen's YouTube channel: www.youtube.com/user/JaenRafael/videos.

Burn and Dodge Modalities in Photoshop Costume Renderings[2]

The Burn and Dodge modalities can be useful painting techniques when creating depth and shape by inserting shadows and highlights into the costume sketch layers. The steps below will guide you in effectively using these tools.

Burn Steps

1. Open the character sketch (that you intend to edit) in Photoshop. You can enlarge the image, to better see what you are doing, by pressing [Command] + [+] or by going to View > Zoom in the upper (computer screen) menu.

2. Select the Eyedropper tool from your left side tool column.

3. Sample the area you intend to edit. In the sample case, I will start with the face.

4. Open the color palette (Color Picker: Foreground Color). It will now be based around the sampled skin tone.

5. While in the Color Picker, move the small circle indicator and select a darker color shade within the skin tone palette.

6. Next, switch to the Brush tool.

7. Set the Mode (upper tool row) to Color Burn. This setting adds a wonderful texture, almost like adding blush or bronzer to a skin tone, or mixing ink to watercolors.

8. Set the Opacity to a low percentage, e.g., 15% or less.

9. Using the drop-down menu, next to the Brush icon on the upper left tool row, choose a soft, well-sized brush for your task—think of it like adding makeup with a brush.

10. Using the brush, add the Burn color to the face. It will look like makeup or shadows (see Figure 6.1).

11. Remember to SAVE the new changes by going to [File] > [SAVE AS] > [Sketch Name] in the upper tool interface row of your computer screen.

Dodge Steps

1. To add highlights to the face and hair, change the selected color to a lighter tint within the Color Picker window.

2. Set Brush Mode to Color Dodge. This is the opposite of Color Burn; instead of burning the image, it will bleach it.

3. Lower the Opacity to 10% or less. Test it—you can bleach more color out by brushing the desired area repeated times.

FIGURE 6.1

In this example, I found a color, in Burn modality, that worked well with various layers, including the hair when it was set at a higher Opacity.

4. You can use the same process to add highlights to the character's hair (see Figure 6.2).

5. You can add highlights to the skin as well. Do not be afraid if it seems as though you are adding a bit too much, because once you decrease the size of the screen image, it will look fine. You can decrease the image size by pressing [Command] + [+] or by going to View > Zoom in the upper (computer screen) menu.

6. Remember to SAVE the new changes by going to [File] > [SAVE AS] > [Sketch Name] in the upper tool interface row of your computer screen.

Painting Eyes

1. Choose the color that you want to use to paint the eyes.

2. Select the Paint Bucket tool.

3. Set the Mode to Normal.

4. Set the Opacity to 100%.

5. Using the Paint Bucket, dump the color inside the eyeball. If you need to, zoom in with [Command] > [+]—you may find mistakes you never noticed before, which you can easily repair now.

6. If dumping the color with Paint Bucket does not work, you can switch to the Brush tool and draw the color in by hand (see Figure 6.3). One of the reasons it may not be working is that the other layers have not had their "white" thoroughly erased in the specific layer. If this is the case, draw the color into the "white" area of the topmost layer.

7. Switch Mode to Color Burn.

8. Change Opacity to a low level, e.g., 10%.

9. With the Brush tool, outline around the bottom of the eyes.

10. Next, switch the Mode to Normal.

11. Change color to a black, and add pupils with the Brush tool.

12. Change color to a white, and add bright, reflective points (see Figure 6.4).

13. Remember to SAVE the new changes by going to [File] > [SAVE AS] > [Sketch Name] in the upper tool interface row of your computer screen.

Touch-Up Work

1. Choose the Brush tool, and then select the Eyedropper tool and sample the (already applied) burn-tone on the skin.

2. Choose a slightly darker tone in the Color Picker palette.

3. Switch the Mode to Color Burn, and set the Opacity to about 30%.

4. Add some makeup (eyeliner or smoky shadow) to the eyes.

5. Choose a larger brush and lower the Opacity to 15% or less.

6. Using the brush, paint some shadows in the area around the brow, eyes, and nose (see Figure 6.5).

7. Next, choose a color for the lips.

8. Make the Brush tool an appropriate size by using the drop-down menu (Size and Hardness) next to the Brush icon on the upper tool row and then paint the lips.

9. You can make the upper lip a shade or two darker than the lower lip.

10. Next, lighten the color by choosing a softer tint in the Color Picker dialogue window and paint highlights (at 100%) with the brush. This step will add a glossy texture to the lips as desired.

FIGURE 6.2

Use the Dodge modality to add highlights to the character's hair.

FIGURE 6.3

If dumping the color with Paint Bucket is not working, you can switch to the Brush tool and draw the color in by hand.

FIGURE 6.4

In Normal mode, change the eye color to white, and add bright and reflective points.

FIGURE 6.5

Using the Brush, paint some Burn shadows in the area around the brow, eyes, and nose.

11. Zoom out with [Command] > [-].

12. View the new depth of the character's features (see Figure 6.6).

13. Remember to SAVE the new changes by going to [File] > [SAVE AS] > [Sketch Name] in the upper tool interface row of your computer screen.

Painting Hair and Adding Real Hair Images[3]

Steps

1. Create a Hair layer using the Lasso tool to select, copy, and paste in the new Hair layer.

2. Duplicate the Hair layer—to rework it later as needed, when it is SAVED.

3. Pick a mid-tone hair color (use safe for printing Only Web Colors, found in the bottom left box), or select colors based on HSB or RGB color models (see Figure 6.7).

4. Dump the color in the Hair layer using the Paint Bucket.

5. Select the Burn and Dodge tools on the top row interface menu.

6. Add basic shade and highlights using Burn and Dodge respectively as described in the previous example (see Figure 6.8).

7. Keep the Burn tool at 50% or less, and match real hair's dark tones.

8. Choose a light tint for the Dodge tool (15% or less).

9. To add contrast and detail, pick a darker shade of the base color to use with the Brush tool—I find a medium-size square sponge shape is best. Keep the Burn brush mode at 50% or less, and the Dodge at 15% or less (see Figure 6.9).

10. To keep the highlights inside the hair's shape, close all the other layers except for the Hair layer. Apply the Magic Wand by choosing [Select] > [Reverse] to isolate the hair shape. Next, use the Brush tool inside the pulsating area to add the desired contrast and detail. This way there won't be any color bleeding onto the areas outside of the hair shape, which seem invisible now but may show up in the final sketch if not contained.

11. Remember to SAVE the new changes by going to [File] > [SAVE AS] > [Sketch Name] in the upper tool interface row of your computer screen.

Another option is to cut and paste a real hair image using the Lasso tool. Review the steps below.

1. Open the layer in your sketch that you want to use, and the image with your hair sample.

2. Using the Magic Lasso, outline the hair from the hair sample image (see Figure 6.10).

3. Copy the hair sample image, and then paste it on top of the Face layer or other desired drawing/sketch layer. You can name it "Real Hair."

4. In your top row tool interface menu click [Image] > [Free Transform].

5. Work with the image to create the desired shape and size, and pivot the image until the hair is positioned in the right direction.

6. Make sure that the image is copied as an under-layer to your drawing. If it is not, click and drag it below the B & W Silhouette layer corresponding to hair in your Photoshop layer windows.

7. Using the Eraser tool, give the image a "haircut" by erasing the parts outside your character's hairline outline (see Figures 6.11 and 6.12).

FIGURE 6.6

Review the new depth of the character's features.

Pick a mid-tone hair color; use safe for printing "Only Web Colors" (botton left box) or select colors based on HSB or RGB color models

FIGURE 6.7

Pick a mid-tone hair color (use safe for printing Only Web Colors, found in the Color Picker bottom left box). Model: Actress Ephie Aardema (as Peggy Sawyer), for the show *42nd Street*, at Stoneham Theatre in MA, May 5–29, 2011. The artistic support team included Ilyse Robbins (directing and choreography), Kathryn Kawecki (scenic design), Rafael Jaen (costume design), Jeff Adelberg (lighting design), Sarah Rozen (props), and pianist Jim Rice (musical director).

FIGURE 6.8

Add basic shade and highlights using Burn and Dodge, respectively.

Next, pick the brush modes: 50% or less "Burn" for the darkers areas

FIGURE 6.9

To add contrast and detail, pick a darker shade of the base color.

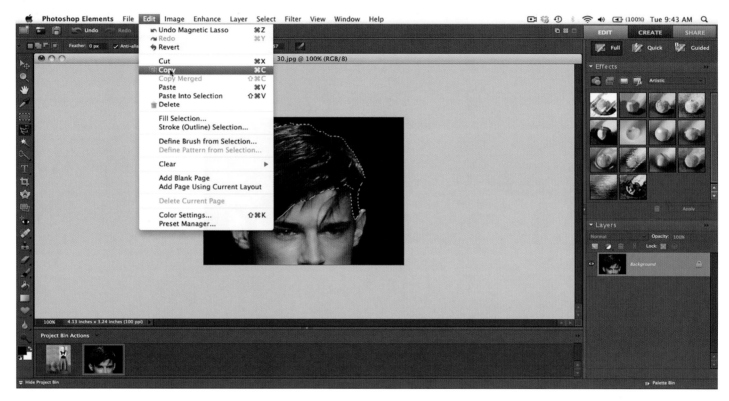

FIGURE 6.10

Using the Magic Lasso, outline the hair from the sample image that you have chosen.

FIGURE 6.11

Using the Eraser tool, give the image a haircut by erasing the excess hair.

FIGURE 6.12

Neaten the shape by erasing the parts outside your character's hairline.

8. With the proper size Brush tool, fill in the white areas using a matching hair color (which you can sample with the Eyedropper tool).

9. Note: Check that the layer you are painting is the layer you can fill in—sometimes the spot you're noticing is actually a white patch on another layer.

10. Remember to label the new layer—in this case, Hair layer.

11. Voila! We have a realistic hair layer! This is important to the designer whose design concept is based on textures.

12. Remember to SAVE the new changes by going to [File] > [SAVE AS] > [Sketch Name] in the upper tool interface row of your computer screen.

Adding Patterns with Movement[4]

Steps

1. Open the Black & White character sketch.

2. Go to the layer that you intend to edit.

3. Click on the Paint tool, and choose "Pattern." Click on a SAVED or "prepared" pattern in the drop-down upper tool row interface menu. In this case, "prepared" means that the pattern design is like a tile, and the left and right sides of the pattern swatch, as well as the top and bottom, will fit to each other seamlessly—like an actual, real-life design (done with tiles) that fills the fabric yardage of the article of clothing. An example is when a flower at the top of a design is cut off, and it is completed by the small stem piece showing over the pattern's bottom.

4. If necessary, adjust size of design to match your needs.

5. Switch layers back to your B & W Silhouette Sketch.

6. Select the Paint Bucket tool, and "Pattern." Make sure to select the Photoshop pattern you intend to dump into the skirt layer (see Figure 6.13).

7. Fill the skirt with the new pattern (see Figure 6.14).

8. If you or the director wanted a chiffon fabric overlay as part of the costume, you would create a new layer.

9. Duplicate the B & W Silhouette (outline) layer.

10. Change label to "Overlay." In the video example, I call it "Skirt Overlay."

11. Drag the new layer above the existing piece—like an actual chiffon overlay would be above the skirt fabric on an existing skirt.

12. Lower the layer's Opacity on the lower right side interface column until it has the desired amount of transparency, e.g., 45–50%. You may want to adjust this again later in the process (see Figure 6.15).

13. Next, select the Paint Bucket tool in "Pattern" mode.

14. Select the Photoshop pattern you desire.

15. Now dump the pattern design into the chiffon layer.

16. In order to create a color match that goes with your palette (in real life you would dye the chiffon fabric), you will have to use the Burn and Dodge modalities to find the right fabric color tones.

17. To find the right chiffon fabric color (see Figure 6.16), switch to the Skirt layer and then select the Eyedropper tool to sample the colors that you desire.

18. Next, switch back to chiffon layer.

19. Select Brush tool.

20. Experiment to find the right size of the brush. Some Photoshop versions get a circle showing the size of the brush, some only show an X, and so experimentation is often necessary.

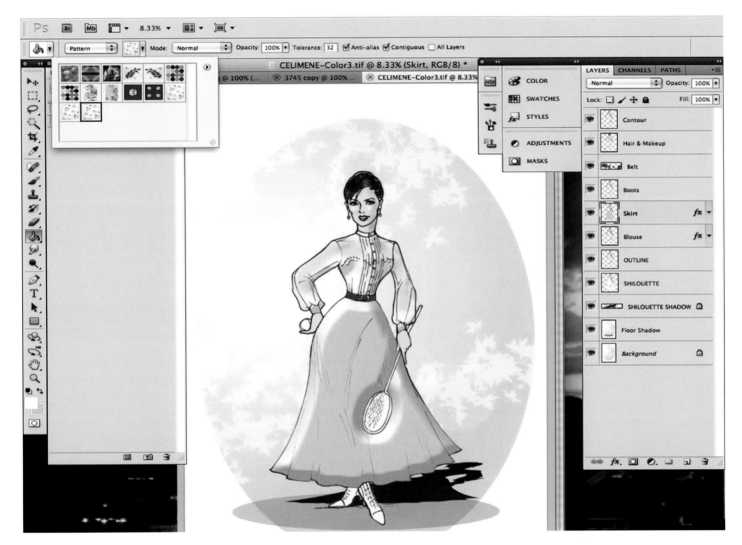

FIGURE 6.13

Make sure to select the pattern you intend to dump into the garment.

FIGURE 6.14

Fill the chosen garment with the new pattern.

FIGURE 6.15

Lower Opacity until it has the desired amount of transparency. (You may want to adjust this again later in the process.)

FIGURE 6.16

To find the right chiffon fabric color, switch to the Skirt layer, and select the Eyedropper tool to sample the color you desire.

21. After you have found the proper brush, lower the color Opacity (upper tool row).

22. Begin to add burning lines to the costume until you feel as though the contrast in the garment's fold is acceptable.

23. Next, select the Color Dodge mode.

24. Open your Color Picker palette, and select a lighter color.

25. Using the Brush tool, add the desired highlights to the costume.

26. Play with the Opacity levels if the highlight seems too strong. Sometimes I lower it to 15% and use the Brush tool a few times till I get the intensity I want.

27. Now you have a new chiffon layer over your costume.

28. Remember to SAVE the new changes by going to [File] > [SAVE AS] > [Sketch Name] in the upper tool interface row of your computer screen.

Adding Floor Shadows[5]

In order to give an impression of what happens on stage, in a real live theatre, we will focus on one general floor shadow and one specific silhouette shadow, as opposed to the different angles and shadows a lighting designer may create on the stage floor.

Steps

1. Open the costume sketch that you intend to edit.

2. Open the Layers toolbar, and the Undo History toolbar, using the drop-down menu in your computer screen upper banner—Window > Layers and Window > (undo) History.

3. We'll work on the Template (background) layer and Black & White Silhouette (Outline) layer, so let's

make all other layers invisible by clicking the Eye icon beside their pictures on the Layers toolbar.

4. Duplicate the Template (background) layer by double-clicking or right-clicking the image layer on the Layer toolbar.

5. Name the new layer Floor Shadow.

6. Duplicate the Black & White Silhouette (Outline) layer.

7. Name this new layer Silhouette Shadow.

8. Arrange (drag) the layers, located in the right side column interface, from top to bottom as follows:

   a. Black & White Silhouette (Outline) layer

   b. Silhouette Shadow

   c. Floor Shadow

   d. Template (background)

9. Select Floor Shadow layer.

10. Double-click (or right-click) the Marquee tool in your left side tool column interface, and select the "Elliptical" shape option (see Figure 6.17).

11. Place an ellipsis underneath the character's feet.

12. Select Paint Bucket tool.

13. Select a shadowy-gray color in your Color Picker window.

14. Set the Mode to Normal and make the Opacity about 45–50%.

15. Fill the ellipsis. If it is too dark, you can change the layer's Opacity itself by selecting it on the Layer's toolbar, going to the top right corner of the toolbar, and lowering the Opacity percentage.

16. You will now see an example of a generic shadow from a top-down light in the sketch's floor (see Figure 6.18).

17. Next, switch to the Silhouette Shadow layer, and hide the B & W Silhouette, the Floor Shadow, and the Template (background) layers.

18. You can use two different options for the next step:

    a. Select the Magic Wand tool on the left side tool column interface, click outside the image, and then go to [Select] > [Inverse].

    OR

    b. After selecting the layer that you'll be working on, click on the Lock icon located on the right side of the Layer itself—the Lock is opposite to the Eye icon. This will allow you to paint the image without going out onto the transparent pixels.

19. Select the Brush tool.

20. Paint with the same color (as in previous steps) but with a 100% Opacity, keeping it in the Normal mode.

21. Paint over the silhouette (see Figure 6.19).

22. Next, go to the computer's upper menu and choose [Image] > [Transform] > [Free Transform]. In some Creative Suite versions, the "Transform" option is under "Edit."

23. After the rectangular frame appears, drag the top of the Silhouette Shadow towards the sketch's floor, and save the changes by clicking "Enter" or choosing the green checkmark that will appear in the dialogue window as you exit the image.

24. Make the Silhouette layer visible by clicking on the Eye icon.

25. Go back to the Silhouette Shadow layer.

26. Go to [Image] > [Transform] > [Free Transform].

27. Drag the shadow until the feet align with those on the B & W Silhouette layer.

28. Go to [Image] > [Transform] > [Perspective]. In Creative Suite, you may have more options, such as Skew, Warp, Distort, etc.

29. A rectangular frame will appear; you can drag the corners of it to angle the shadow on the stage floor away from the imaginary light source. This directionality will add another feeling of depth.

30. Continue to shift or play around with your shadow's position to change the perspective until you are satisfied (see Figure 6.20).

31. Make all four of the layers that you've worked with visible.

32. If the floor shadow is too far removed from the Silhouette shadow, follow the steps below:

    a. Go back to the Floor Shadow layer.

    b. Re-select the Marquee tool with an ellipsis shape.

    c. Create a larger shadow shape over the original floor shadow.

    d. Fill in the new shadow with the same color and they will blend into one, larger floor shadow (see Figure 6.21).

33. Make all other Photoshop layers visible again to see your character under the new lighting.

34. Go to the Floor Shadow layer.

35. Go to [Filter] > [Render] > [Lens Flare] OR [Lighting Effects]. Note: For the purposes of the example, I selected [Lens Flare].

36. A dialogue interface window toolbar should open for Lens Flare.

37. Create a spotlight, with a customizable amount of brightness. Note: In the video example, I set the spotlight to the Floor Shadow layer, which had its

FIGURE 6.17

Double-click (or right-click) the Marquee tool and select the elliptical shape, then place an ellipsis underneath the character's feet.

FIGURE 6.18

Suggestion of a top-down light in the sketch's floor.

FIGURE 6.19

Paint with the same color (as in previous steps) but with a 100% Opacity, keeping it in the Normal mode.

FIGURE 6.20

Angle your shadow to add directionality to the light source, and to create a different sense of depth.

FIGURE 6.21

Fill in the new shadow with the same color, and they will blend into one larger floor shadow.

overall Opacity set to 45%; after creating the same spotlight effect on the Background layer, it was much stronger.

38. Customize the brightness of the spotlight to suit your needs.

39. Select the Elliptical Marquee tool again.

40. Create an elliptical frame around your character.

41. Go to [Select] > [Inverse].

42. Select color—I chose white in the video example.

43. Select the Paint Bucket tool with 100% Opacity.

44. If you do not like the transparency that comes with this frame, follow these steps:

    a. Select the Floor Shadow layer.

    b. Dump the color with the Paint Bucket tool again.

45. Press "Enter" or select the Marquee tool and click on the picture to SAVE it (see Figure 6.22).

46. Remember to SAVE the new changes by going to [File] > [SAVE AS] > [Sketch Name] in the upper tool interface row of your computer screen.

Using Bevel and Emboss to Add Dimension to the Character's Silhouette[6]

Steps

1. Open the Costume sketch that you want to work on.

2. Select the Photoshop (garment) layer that you're editing.

3. Select the Magic Wand tool.

4. While holding the [Shift] key, click on (select) the entire character, as well as the spaces bordered by her/his body parts.

5. Go to your computer's upper row interface and choose [Select] > [Inverse]. This step will isolate the actual silhouette of the character.

6. Click on the "Fx" (effects) symbol in the Layers toolbar. Note: It may be at the bottom or at the top of the interface window, depending on your Photoshop version.

7. Choose Bevel and Emboss in the drop-down menu.

8. Next, an interface dialogue window should open. Make sure that Bevel and Emboss are still checked in the options inside the dialogue window.

9. Under "Structure," play with "Size," "Soften," and "Depth" to create a three-dimensional rise on the edge of your selected silhouette. You should be able to immediately see the change on your actual sketch's silhouette (see Figure 6.23).

10. Under "Shading," play with Opacity and types under "Highlight Mode" and "Shadow Mode."

11. Select "New Style" and save it—this step will make the process easier later (Step #16).

12. Now, press "OK" to save your changes.

13. Select the Blouse layer.

14. Select the "Fx" symbol again and then choose Bevel and Emboss.

15. Select the "Style" tab on the top left of the "Layer Style" window.

16. Select the style you SAVED in Step #11.

17. Now, assess the effects on your Blouse layer.

18. If you find the bevel is too light or dark, double-click the "Fx" symbol while on the Blouse layer, and edit the "Shading" effects. Select "OK" to save your changes (see Figure 6.24).

FIGURE 6.22

If you do not like the transparency that comes with this frame, select the Floor Shadow layer and dump color in it with the Paint Bucket.

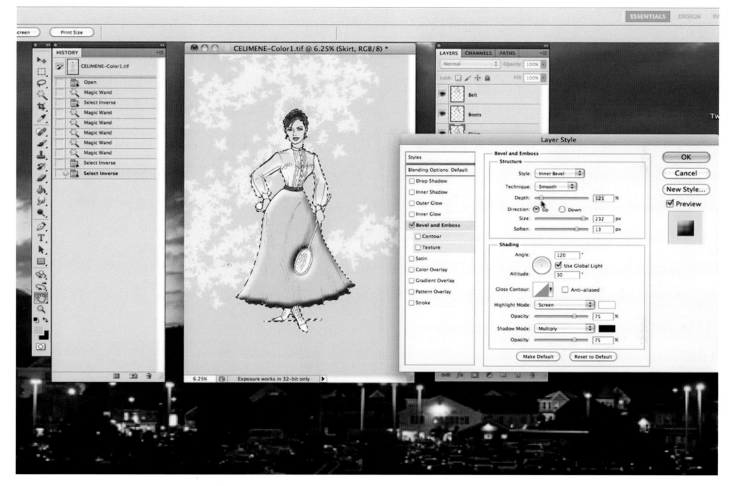

FIGURE 6.23

Under "Structure," play with Size, Soften, and Depth to create a three-dimensional rise on the edge of your selected silhouette.

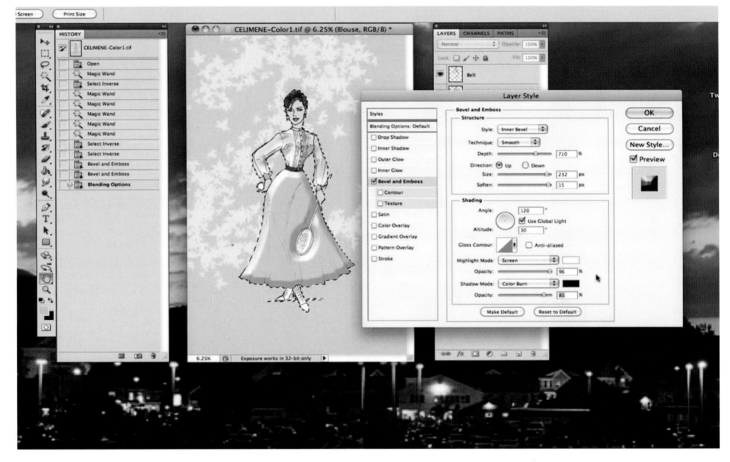

FIGURE 6.24

If you find the bevel is too light or dark, double-click the Fx symbol now on the Blouse layer, and edit the "Shading" effects.

19. Select Marquee tool, and click on the sketch to get rid of the outline.

20. Save your edits going to [File] > [SAVE AS . . .]. You can save the updated sketch as both a Photoshop (for editing) and a JPEG (for printing) file.

21. Tip: A good way to stay organized is to number each of your "saves."

22. Remember to SAVE the new changes by going to [File] > [SAVE AS] > [Sketch Name] in the upper tool interface row of your computer screen.

Testimonial 1

BRIDGET KATHLEEN O'LEARY—ASSOCIATE ARTISTIC DIRECTOR AND DIRECTOR

Designers see and hear the world of the play in rich layers . . .

Bio

Bridget Kathleen O'Leary is the Associate Artistic Director at New Repertory Theatre where she has directed productions of *Scenes from an Adultery*, *Muckrakers*, *Pattern of Life*, *Lungs*, *Fully Committed*, *Collected Stories*, *Dollhouse*, *boom*, *Charles Dickens' A Christmas Carol*, and *Fool for Love*. Other directing credits include: *The Other Place* for the Nora Theatre Company and Underground Railway Theater; *Recent Tragic Events* and *Aunt Dan and Lemon* for Whistler in the Dark Theatre; and *Reconsidering Hanna(h)* and *The Devil's Teacup* at Boston Playwrights' Theatre. In 2007, she assisted Artistic Director Wendy C. Goldberg at the National Playwrights' Conference at the Eugene O'Neill Theater Center and worked as an assistant on new plays by Rebecca Gilman and Roberto Aguirre-Sacasa. Before moving to Boston, Bridget worked in Washington, D.C. Since 2012, Bridget has curated the Next Voices Reading Series, a program she established for New Repertory Theatre. She serves as the Chair of the Literary Committee for the National New Play Network and is a member of the New England New Play Alliance. Bridget received her MFA in directing at Boston University.

Interview

Rafael: What are your beliefs (or approach) in regard to collaborating with designers?

Bridget: When I first approach a production, I love to get the entire design team together in one room and just talk about the play. I think it's as important that I have a vision as it is that I remain open to others. How do they see the world of the play, the characters? What is the story to them? Designers see and hear the world of the play in rich layers and it always influences my rehearsal process.

Rafael: What are your beliefs (or approach) in regard to collaborating with costume designers?

Bridget: I think it's important for the director to have a strong vision, but I love the new ideas and imagery that the designers bring to the table.

Design Gallery: *Dollhouse*, a drama by Theresa Rebeck, based on Henrik Ibsen's *A Doll's House*

Set in suburban Connecticut, this contemporary adaptation of Ibsen's classic follows the iconic Nora as she struggles to preserve her seemingly perfect life. Nora's 'happy home' is compromised when a man from her past unexpectedly resurfaces and threatens to reveal her secret. In this play by critically acclaimed playwright Theresa Rebeck, Nora must decide between her idyllic world and a life she can truly claim as her own. Based on Henrik Ibsen's *A DOLL'S HOUSE.*[7]

FIGURE 6.25

Sarah Newhouse and Will Lyman in *Dollhouse* by Theresa Rebeck. Bridget Kathleen O'Leary, director; Kathryn Kawecki, scenic designer; Rafael Jaen, costume designer; Chris Brusberg, lighting design; Scott Nason, sound designer; Julie Tidemand, properties supervisor; Victoria S. Coady, production stage manager. New Repertory Theatre, 2011.

FIGURE 6.26

Sample Fashion Style Sheet for *Dollhouse*. New Repertory Theatre, 2011. Digital Tools: Collage in Google Slides.

New Repertory Theater, February 2011
Directed by Bridget O'Leary
Costume Ideas by Rafael Jaen

NORA

DOLL HOUSE

Naïve, Sheltered, Sophisticated, Entitled, "Ghost of Christmas Past"

New Repertory Theater, February 2011
Directed by Bridget O'Leary
Costume Ideas by Rafael Jaen

EVAN

HOUSE

Recovering, Ambitious, Stubborn, Objectifying, Status Quo

FIGURE 6.27

Sample Fashion Style Sheet for *Dollhouse*. New Repertory Theatre, 2011. Digital Tools: Collage in Google Slides.

Testimonial 2

CARMEL O'REILLY—ARTISTIC DIRECTOR, DIRECTOR, AND ACTOR

It is important to leave space that allows for the serendipitous discoveries that may emerge organically from the rehearsal process.

Bio

Carmel O'Reilly has directed numerous productions in the New England area over the past 25 years with many theatre companies, including the A.R.T, New Rep, Speakeasy Stage, Gloucester Stage, WHAT, Lyric Stage, and others. She is founder and Artistic Director of the Súgán Theatre Company, for which she directed many Elliot Norton award-winning productions. She has directed at several area colleges including Harvard, Emerson, and Boston College, where she was the Monan Visiting Professor in Theatre Arts in 2010. Most recently she directed Jimmy Titanic for Tir Na Theatre Company that toured to NYC, Philadelphia, Santa Barbara, Dublin, Belfast, and other venues.

Interview

Rafael: What are your beliefs (or approach) in regard to collaborating with designers?

Carmel: Beyond the fundamental design elements that are usually conceived and agreed upon during the early stages of a production, it is important to leave space that allows for the serendipitous discoveries that may emerge organically from the rehearsal process.

Rafael: What are your beliefs (or approach) in regard to collaborating with costume designers?

Carmel: In particular, the costume designer should remain engaged with the actors as they develop their characters. Changing perspectives does not mean surrendering to capricious whims nor compromising brilliant designs, but exploring or expanding ideas with the actor and the director. In the same vein, the attention of the costume designer to the myriad details that surface in the dress rehearsal period is of singular importance. Such attention to detail, in tandem with the rest of the creative team, completes the design signature.

Design Gallery: *The Seafarer*

Both hilarious and chilling, *The Seafarer* weaves a mythic tale of the sea,
Ireland, and redemption. On Christmas Eve in North Dublin, Sharky Harkin
finds himself reluctantly hosting old friends at the dingy house he shares
with his brother who has recently gone blind. A lot of booze and
card-playing carry the men into Christmas Day when Sharky must face
the grim promise he made decades ago to one of these old friends.[8]

FIGURE 6.28

Cast: Billy Meleady (James "Sharky" Harkin), Bob Colonna (Richard Harkin), Larry Coen (Ivan Curry), Ciaran Crawford (Nicky Giblin), and Derry Woodhouse (Mr. Lockhart). Production
Staff: Written by Conor McPherson, Directed by Carmel O'Reilly, Scenic Design by J. Michael Griggs, Costume Design by Rafael Jaen, Lighting Design by John R Malinowski, Sound Design by
Benjamin Emerson, Stage Management by Maureen Lane.

FIGURE 6.29

Sketch for Mr Lockhart for *The Seafarer*, Speakeasy Theatre Company, Winter 2008. Photoshop tools: Brush in Dissolve, Burn, and Dodge modalities.

FIGURE 6.30

Sketch for Richard and Sharky for *The Seafarer*, Speakeasy Theatre Company, Winter 2008. Photoshop tools: Brush in Dissolve, Burn, and Dodge modalities.

Citations and Sources

1 Merriam-Webster. Accessed August 29, 2016. www.merriam-webster.com/dictionary/finished.

2 Jaen, Rafael. "Using Photoshop"s Burn and Dodge Modalities in Costume Renderings." YouTube. 2015. Accessed August 31, 2016. www.youtube.com/watch?v=A7GAsComB9I.

3 Jaen, Rafael. "Digital Costume Rendering—Painting Hair—YouTube." YouTube. 2011. Accessed August 31, 2016. www.youtube.com/watch?v=gWaQSU7mxG0.

4 Jaen, Rafael. "Adding Patterns and Movements to Costume Sketches Using Photoshop." YouTube. 2015. Accessed August 31, 2016. www.youtube.com/watch?v=VPPtZxkHZCE.

5 Jaen, Rafael. "Adding Floor Shadows and Such to Costume Sketches Using Photoshop." YouTube. 2015. Accessed August 31, 2016. www.youtube.com/watch?v=7C9HdSnlr9Y.

6 Jaen, Rafael. "Using Photoshop's Bevel and Emboss in Costume Renderings." YouTube. 2015. Accessed August 31, 2016. www.youtube.com/watch?v=N8LIXIzysFE.

7 "*Dollhouse*—New Repertory Theatre." New Repertory Theatre. Accessed September 01, 2016. www.newrep.org/productions/dollhouse/.

8 "The Seafarer | SpeakEasy." SpeakEasy. Accessed September 01, 2016. www.speakeasystage.com/the-seafarer/.

AT THE CLICK OF A MOUSE, IT'S POSSIBLE TO SEND FRAME GRABS FROM

A MOVIE, SHARE PINTEREST BOARDS OF IMAGES AND IDEAS, VIEW CLIPS

AND TRAILERS ON-LINE – ALL TO AID IN THE CREATIVE DISCUSSION AS THE

CREATIVE VISION EVOLVES FROM BRAINSTORM TO 'BUY IT!'

CATHLEEN O'CONNELL, FILM PRODUCER

CHAPTER 7

ARCHIVING THE PROJECT AS A DIGITAL PORTFOLIO

One benefit of using digital software and Web-sharing tools is that projects get instantly archived during the process. Web folders become our record keeping, giving easy access to files when we need them.

Websites and Photo slideshows can be shared via a link. The result is a presentation that is accessible, practical and convenient for sharing one's work. Many producers and directors can preview the work of a designer/ technician from a website, flash drive, or email PDF file, and this can lead to interviews.

Digital Web archives are appealing because they become practical in the long run: "user-friendly websites are easy to maintain [and] digital files make it easy to share information with fellow designers, technicians, directors, producers, managers, school programs, etc."[1]

Costume Design and Manufacturing for PBS/WGBH

Designing costumes for a film is a 24/7 proposition and the turnaround time is fast. A typical week can start with sketching first thing Monday morning, and emailing JPEGs to producers, production collaborators, and directors by noon. After notes and revisions, an email with images goes to the rental houses and renderings with fabrics go to drapers (if build) early the next day. Subsequently, choices are vetted via email or phone, FedEx accounts and POs are set, orders are placed, the crew is prepped, costumes arrive by Thursday afternoon, and the "star" fittings take place, then scenes are shot on Friday and Saturday. Strike and packing take place on Sunday, and drop-offs in the mail (or store) take place on Monday first thing . . . while we are starting all over again!

Due to the speedy nature of the tasks, compiling materials digitally and across multiple platforms is beneficial to effective communication and collaboration in film. Since schedules can shift and change, the approach also aids in staying organized. In 2009, I had the privilege to work on a PBS documentary. I used the digital approach and in the process, I created a digital portfolio to use as a reference in future projects (see Figures 7.1–7.3).

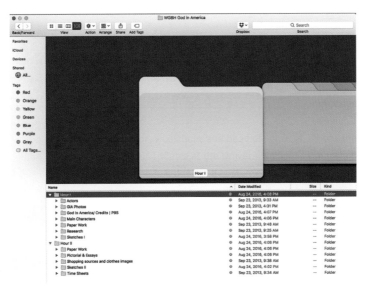

FIGURE 7.1

Digital (Dropbox) Costume "Bible" for the movie *God in America*.

FIGURE 7.2

Thomas Jefferson's Digital Costume Piece List for the movie *God in America*.

| | WGBH: God in America HR 2 | | | | Costume Piece List by: Rafael Jaen | | |

Sizes	Name and Meassurements	Character and Ensemble Roles	Total	Piece List	Vendor	Budget	Total
		Thomas Jefferson Note: 1 Look in office	1	Undershirt	EM	$0.00	
				Ruffle Shirt	jas-townsend.com	$55.00	
Height		He was very private/secretive about his personal beliefs. Confident, intellectual, introverted, a young but old soul.		Waistcoat (vest)	Museum Replicas or Jas-townsend	$120.00	
		Jefferson is seen cutting out a Bible. Much of the time we watch Jefferson through the lattice work of his cut up Bible pages. A craftsman at work... There is a glass encased clock prominently situated, through which we often look – the clock's mechanism in the foreground, the shadowed figure of Jefferson in the background. Pg. 2					
Weight				Breeches	Tudorshop	$75.00	
Chest/Bust				White Stockings	Fugawee.com	$13.00	
Waist				Concord Shoes	Fugawee.com	$110.00	
Suit/ Dress				Stock or Cravat?	EM	$0.00	
Shirt/ Blouse							
Shoes							
		Samples: Cotton ruffle shirt worn by men of status, waiscoat, and period shoes. Notes: The gold waiscoat is available right away from Tudor Shop, a navy or black from Jas-townsend would need a 3 to 4 week lead. Questions: Is the shirt worn and/or dirty? Do we see his shoes?				Sub-total $373.00	$373.00

Page 1   11/11/16

| | WGBH: God in America HR 2 | | | | Costume Piece List by: Rafael Jaen | | |

Sizes	Name and Meassurements	Character and Ensemble Roles	Total	Piece List	Vendor	Budget	Total
		Archbishop Hughes	1	Undershirt	EM	$0.00	
				Priest Shirt	Shirt	$0.00	
		We find John Hughes at 55, looking back at his fight against the Protestant establishment in New York City. A lean muscular man, he looked more like a well-tailored fighter than a clergyman—he developed a habit of spreading into a vee the top buttons of his Roman collar. Thunderous fighter, violent yet compassionate, intolerant for intolerance, introvert in the public eye.		Pontif Collar	ChristianBook.com	$12.00	
				Cassock	Murphys Robes	$350.00	
Height		Hughes stands brooding at the end of a jetty. Pg. 29		Chasuble or Surplice (White Robe)	Murphys Robes	$90.00	
Weight		Hughes dresses for communion. Pg. 34		Red Stole	Murphys Robes	$75.00	
Chest/Bust							
Waist				Mitre Hat?	EM	$0.00	
				Black w/red pipping Band			
Suit/ Dress				Cinture	Murphys Robes	$80.00	
Shirt/ Blouse				Knicker Pants	EM	$0.00	
Shoes				Stockings	EM	$0.00	
				Shoes	EM	$0.00	
		Samples: Wool blend (fully lined) House Cassock with red pipping and buttons. Black and red band cintura (waist sash). Questions: I am thinking that adding a white Surplice (over robe) and red stole (scarf) will work as his pulpit outfit? Or we could use the white Chasuble (poncho) with the red stole. I am staying away from $150 Mitre Hat. Does he need a neck cross?				Sub-total $607.00	$607.00

Page 2   11/11/16

FIGURE 7.3

Archbishop Hughes' Digital Costume Piece List for the movie *God in America*.

American Experience: *God in America*
(Parts 1 and 2), Fall 2010

A documentary with historical re-enactments, directed by David Belton and produced by Front Line executive producers and award-winning documentary filmmakers. It was a privilege working on this movie. The team included outstanding professionals and "A"-list actors. I interviewed for the job in early May 2009 and got hired a week later to design the first part of the film. Award-winning director David Belton hired me because of my historical research and the emotion that I brought to my designs.

***God in America* is a timely examination of the potent and complex interaction between religion and democracy, the origins of the American concept of religious liberty, and the controversial evolution of that ideal in the nation's courts and political arena. It also explores the intersection of political struggle and spiritual experience in the lives of key American historical figures including Franciscan Friars and the Pueblo leader Po'pay, Puritan leader John Winthrop and dissident Anne Hutchinson, Catholic Bishop John Hughes, abolitionist Frederick Douglass, President Thomas Jefferson and contemporary leaders.**

Interweaving documentary footage, historical dramatization, and interviews with religious historians, the six-part series is narrated by actor Campbell Scott and includes appearances by actors Michael Emerson (as John Winthrop), Chris Sarandon (as Abraham Lincoln), and Keith David (as Frederick Douglass), amongst others. 'The American story cannot be fully understood without understanding the country's religious history,' says series executive producer Michael Sullivan.[2]

UK journalist Rachel Ray wrote: "Using dramatic re-enactments, interviews with prominent religion scholars, documentary footage, and photographs, *God in America* goes on to look at how religious belief shaped the origins of the Civil War and President Abraham Lincoln's actions. . . . *God in America* is a meticulous, thoughtful, and provocative production. It is a must-see for anyone who wants to understand the motivations and actions behind America's relentless quest for religious freedom that began almost 400 years ago.[3]

Testimonial 1

Words of Wisdom Regarding Film Production Collaboration

CATHLEEN O'CONNELL—FILM PRODUCER

If you think you are the smartest person in the room, you are in the wrong room.

Bio

Cathleen O'Connell is a documentary producer based in Boston. She has worked on numerous PBS documentaries, many of which feature historical dramatic recreations. Her recent work includes three films for the PBS series American Experience: *The Perfect Crime* (Producer/Director), *War of the Worlds* (Producer/Director), and *Ripley: Believe It or Not* (Producer/Director/Writer). Her other PBS credits include: co-producer for two episodes of *God in America* (a coproduction of American Experience and Frontline), coordinating producer for *We Shall Remain* (a five-part mini-series surveying Native history in America from the 1600s to the 21st century), and recreations producer for *The Latino Americans*. Her independent films include a documentary about Native American marching bands entitled *Sousa on the Rez* and the world's only time capsule documentary, *Time Capsule: Message in a Bottle*. She has also worked in the locations department on several feature films filmed in and around Boston, including *Next Stop Wonderland*.

As part of my research (for this book) I conducted and compiled interviews with various professionals who became my mentors during collaborative processes.

While working in *God in America*, I became close friends with the producer Cathleen O'Connell, and I was inspired by her holistic approach.

I am sharing her teaching points below.

Interview

Rafael: In your experience, what makes for an effective film production collaboration?

Cathleen: The key to an effective film production collaboration is first, last, and always: communication. And it's critical to understand that communication is a two-way street. Communication is not a monologue; rather, it is a conversation. As the producer/director, I share my vision with the creative team—a vision, frankly, which may or may not be fully formed when I present it. After putting my ideas out there (and this step is crucial) I listen to the feedback. There's a saying I abide by — "If you think you are the smartest person in the room, you are in the wrong room." I rely heavily on the professionals I collaborate with to bring their wisdom, experience, and ideas to the table, and to turn the kernel of what may be a half-formed impractical dream into a full fledged, achievable plan.

Rafael: What is your role in producing the story?

Cathleen: My role in producing the story depends on the project. As an independent producer, sometimes I'm hatching the original idea and taking it all the way through to the end. Other times, I'm hired to execute someone else's vision. In either scenario, I consider my #1 job description to create an environment where the people I'm working with can do their own best work. At the end of the day, that is what serves the film best. To me, this means understanding what I'm asking of people (i.e., Is it possible? Is it possible given the schedule and budget? If not, what do we have to adjust?). After everyone is on the same page and the expectations are clear, then I step back and let the professionals do their work.

Rafael: What are your thoughts about collaborating with designers; what do you look for?

Cathleen: In collaborating with designers, I look at the types of projects they've done before. I tend to do a lot of historical/period projects, so I look to see if the designer has done period work before and if they understand the unique demands of the genre (for example—sourcing hard-to-find items, building items from scratch if they don't exist, and doing a *lot* of background research in pre-production). I ask to see their research from previous projects, as this gives me a clue about how they work. If it's a film about the 19th century and they can already speak about the evolution of men's pants from knickers to full length and the related class implications, then I know we are on the right track. I also look to see what their resources are—do they have access to collections and have pre-existing relationships with costume houses? Do they have people that they've worked with before and can they assemble a tight team? Also, film production is stressful—there are long hours, deadlines, and budget constraints. I want to go into that pressure-filled production cauldron with a team who will smile under stress rather than snap—so I look to work with people who can maintain a positive "can-do" attitude under both good and bad conditions. I also look for a designer who understands how clothing, fabrics, and color translate from the set to the screen (my medium). I recently did a project where we shot in color but then drained the color out during editing so the footage would look like a vintage black and white film. This added a degree of difficulty to the wardrobe choices; the designer had to select items in anticipation of how the color and texture of the wardrobe would change downstream in the post-production process (for example, when drained of color, a soft pale green becomes gray, a deep emerald green turns black). Also, I appreciate designers who consider the actors. Wardrobe is an important tool that actors use to practice their craft. Cheap, ill-fitting, uncomfortable clothing impacts an actor's ability to do his or her job. I look for a designer who understands this important relationship and can work within a budget without compromising the materials they are giving the actors to inhabit on set.

Rafael: In today's digital era, what are some of the things that you find helpful when communicating with designers via the World Wide Web?

Cathleen: Certainly the Internet has made gathering reference materials and visual inspiration much easier. From fine art databases maintained by museums, to archival footage and stills collections, visual research that used to require on-site visits can be done in front of a computer screen. And after the material has been collected, it's easy to share and disseminate. At the click of a mouse, it's possible to send frame grabs from a movie, share Pinterest boards of images and ideas, view clips and trailers online—all to aid in the creative discussion as the creative vision evolves from brainstorm to "buy it!" Also, thanks to the Internet, not everyone has to work in the same space at the same time. Very often, my production team is in one location while a department head is working in their studio, perhaps miles away, or even in another state or country, and we connect digitally to work together in a "virtual office." (That being said, it's great to have face-to-face meetings and take field trips to look, touch, and feel clothing

as the creative process unfolds, but it's not always possible.)

Rafael: What advice would you give a young practitioner who is starting to work professionally?

Cathleen: My advice would be to say yes to every opportunity. Intern and volunteer on student and independent projects to gain practical experience (and to expand your résumé). Don't be afraid to start at the bottom—your hard work, good attitude, and diligence *will* be noticed and appreciated. (Remember, too, that a bad attitude will be noted as well!) Consume media—watch plays, screen movies, and see TV shows to learn from the choices that are made in those productions. Choose your career because you love to do it. The hours are long and the work is hard, and not many people get rich. But if you love your work—that is its own best reward.

Rafael: Are there any teaching points or take aways that you have from working in God in America*?*

Cathleen: For many of my projects, I've worked with costume houses remotely (renting and shipping items from Los Angeles or England, for example), but for *God in America*, we pulled much of the wardrobe from a wonderful and deep costume collection at a local university. I distinctly remember a meeting our team had in the bowels of the theatre department, pulling out cloaks and shawls, trying them on, and discussing the merits of different fabrics, colors, and textures. It was not only terrific fun (I seem to recall the (male) director modeling a bonnet at one point) but also a highly productive meeting where, by the end of it, we had made a number of key decisions about the look and feel of the wardrobe design. The first lesson was, there can be great resources in your own backyard—don't overlook them! And secondly, face-to-face meetings and field trips are not only team-building, but they can also move the creative process forward by leaps and bounds. Another lesson—for *God in America*, we had an out-of-state film shoot, but no one from the wardrobe department was available to go. (Besides, it was just one day—what could go wrong?) On the day of the shoot, as I stood in the middle of an old growth forest awkwardly trying to pin together a seam on a leather vest being worn by a very patient actor, I was reminded how awesome, and crucial, the wardrobe department is. I managed not to impale the actor, or myself, but I vowed never again to pretend I could fill the experienced shoes of a real wardrobe professional. Thank you wardrobe departments everywhere for all you do!

Design Gallery: *God in America* (Figures 7.4–7.7)

PBS *God in America* (Episodes 1 and 2) Credits:
Director and Writer David Belton, Co-Producer Episode 1 Cathleen O'Connell, Music Philip Sheppard, Production Design Episode 1 Katha Seidman, Production Design Episode 2 Amy Whitten, Costumes Episodes 1 and 2 Rafael Jaen, Makeup and Hair Joe Rossi.

Testimonial 2

MICHAEL FENNIMORE—FILM AND THEATRE ACTOR, AND THEATRE DIRECTOR

Working with a costume designer who understands my vision while drawing on their own conceptual ideas is paramount to a successful production.

Bio
Michael Fennimore has been teaching at Boston Casting for over ten years. He also teaches acting for the camera at UMass Boston where he is a Senior Lecturer II at the Theatre Arts Department, College of Liberal Arts. He is a Graduate of the American Academy of Dramatic Arts-

NYC. For 25 years, Michael has acted and directed the play *Shear Madness* at the Charles Playhouse in Boston, MA. He first got his SAG card in 1980 and had served as its New England president for nine years. Appearing in numerous commercials and dozens of industrials, Michael received his first TV credit with the show *Spenser: For Hire* and more recently had a recurring role in the Showtime Series *Brotherhood*. Michael has a scene with Christian Bale and Amy Adams in the Academy Award nominated film *American Hustle*.

Interview

Rafael: How do you access the characters in a play when you read it for the first time?

Michael: When first reading a script I not only visualize movement and structure, but I also develop a sense of fabric and texture.

Rafael: How would you describe your collaborative approach when working with costume designers?

Michael: Working with a costume designer who understands my vision while drawing on his or her own conceptual ideas is paramount to a successful production. When directing a play, the chemistry among the actors and the production staff is crucial. I always strive to create an atmosphere where creativity thrives and collaboration is encouraged. The welcoming of new ideas keeps theatre alive.

FIGURE 7.4

Sketch and research for John Winthrop, played by actor Michael Emerson. B & W images were scanned, painted with Photoshop, and then saved as JPEGs. The renderings were dropped into Powerpoint slides formatted as 8.5 x 11 sheets.

FIGURE 7.5

Sketch and research for Anne Hutchinson, played by actress Laila Robins. I also saved the sketches as PDF files for email.

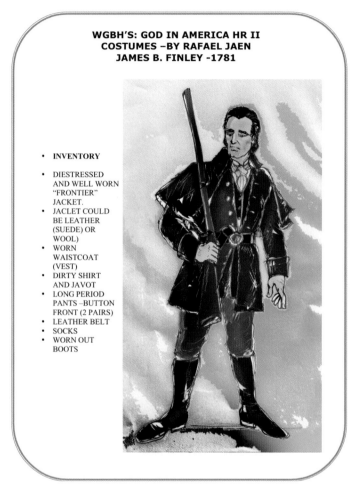

WGBH'S: GOD IN AMERICA HR II
COSTUMES –BY RAFAEL JAEN
JAMES B. FINLEY -1781

- **INVENTORY**

- DIESTRESSED AND WELL WORN "FRONTIER" JACKET.
- JACLET COULD BE LEATHER (SUEDE) OR WOOL)
- WORN WAISTCOAT (VEST)
- DIRTY SHIRT AND JAVOT
- LONG PERIOD PANTS –BUTTON FRONT (2 PAIRS)
- LEATHER BELT
- SOCKS
- WORN OUT BOOTS

FIGURE 7.6

Sketch and research for James B. Finley, played by actor Creighton James.

WGBH'S: GOD IN AMERICA HR II
COSTUMES –BY RAFAEL JAEN
THOMAS JEFFERSON - 1776

- **INVENTORY**

- OFF WHITE WORN JAVOT

- OFF WHITE WORN SHIRT

- CHARCOAL WAISTCOAT

- BLACK KNICKERS

- OFF WHITE HOSE

- CONCORD SHOES

FIGURE 7.7

Sketch and research for Thomas Jefferson, played by actor Byron Jennings.

Design Gallery: *You Can't Take It With You*
(Figures 7.8–7.12)

Because it is a lot of fun. People are going to get so involved. When they walk into the theatre, by the way, 1930s music is going to be playing, you are going to be transported back into the 1930s. The whole time, when there is a scene change, there is going to be music in there. This is a family that basically says people make a living but people don't live. And this is a family that just enjoys life.

Michael Fennimore[4]

FIGURE 7.8

UMass Boston, Theatre Arts, Fall 2014, *You Can't Take It With You*. The cast includes from left to right: Ben Sibley (Boris Kolenkhov), Thomas Koen (Grandpa), Scott Stewardson (Ed), Erin Reilly (Grand Duchess), Alex Texidore (Paul Sycamore), Cassidy Bane (Essie), and Alana Bassett (Pennie). *You Can't Take It With You*. Playwright: George S. Kaufman and Moss Hart, Director: Michael Fennimore, Scenic and Lighting Designer: Anthony Phelps, Costume Designer: Rafael Jaen, Sound Designer: Vanessa Charles, Makeup and Hair Design: Tori Moline, Props Master: Jaime Biancardi, Stage Manager: Lauren Annese.

FIGURE 7.9

Finished sketch for Penny X1 in *You Can't Take It With You*, UMass Boston, Fall 2014. The character silhouette was drawn with a Wacom tablet and then painted using Photoshop. The collaged images were "Lassoed," copied and pasted, and then "Free Transformed." They were painted using brushes in various modalities, adding actual fabric patterns, and Bevel and Emboss.

FIGURE 7.10

Finished sketch for Alice X1, *You Can't Take It With You*, UMass Boston, Fall 2014.

ED
ACT I

You Can't Take
It with You

Directed by Michael Fennimore
Costumes by Rafael Jaen
Fall 2014

UMASS
BOSTON

Mrs. Kirby

You Can't Take
It with You

Directed by Michael Fennimore
Costumes by Rafael Jaen
Fall 2014

UMASS
BOSTON

FIGURE 7.11

Finished sketch for Ed X1, *You Can't Take It With You*, UMass Boston, Fall 2014.

FIGURE 7.12

Finished sketch for Mrs. Kirby X1, *You Can't Take It With You*, UMass Boston, Fall 2014.

Citations and Sources

1   Jaen, Rafael. "Chapter 6: The Effective Digital Portfolio." In *Show Case*, 2nd ed. Waltham, MA: Focal Press, 2011.

2   "Introduction." PBS. October 11, 2010. Accessed August 17, 2016. www.pbs.org/godinamerica/etc/introduction.html.

3   Ray, Rachel. "God in America, PBS: US TV Review." *The Telegraph*. October 08, 2010. Accessed August 17, 2016. www.telegraph.co.uk/culture/tvandradio/8052281/God-in-America-PBS-US-TV-review.html.

4   Posted: Sunday, November 09, 2014 11:33 a.m. "UMass Boston Professor Directs Dysfunctional Comedic Play 'You Can't Take It With You'." Accessed September 01, 2016. http://m.umassmedia.com/mobile/art_lifestyle/umass-boston-professor-directs-dysfunctional-comedic-play-you-can-t/article_9a98bd24-682e-11e4-8f2d-f7b75a72f8a1.html.

CHAPTER 8

TESTIMONIALS ABOUT DIGITAL DESIGN IN COLLABORATION

In my career in regional theatre, film, and academia, I have had the opportunity to share and teach my digital rendering techniques via USITT programing. The Institute's mission is to connect "performing arts design and technology communities to ensure a vibrant dialog among practitioners, educators, and students." As such, the organization has afforded me the privilege of working with extraordinary professionals who continuously educate and inspire me. Many of these colleagues have adapted my digital design approach, serving their personal working styles.

In this chapter, I am sharing "words of wisdom" from practicing professionals with years of experience in the field of costume design. I am also featuring digital costume design images that are a product of their collaborations in different projects. I hope that you find the enclosed information as enlightening as I have.

An Unforgettable Affair with Photoshop
Esther Van Eek

USITT Costume Design and Technology Commission, *Sightlines*, October 2010

The standing ovation at the end of the third day said it all. The large group of tired but enthusiastic participants, whether total neophytes or experienced Photoshop illustrators, had all worked hard for three intense days of instruction, practice, and more practice. Though weary from focusing on computer monitors for hours each day, facing frustration and failure, and more hours finishing homework each evening, participants engaged in the work were spurred on by glimpses of the amazing range of possibilities that Photoshop offers the costume designer.

Rafael Jaen, symposium instructor, designer, and author of two books on creating and maintaining design-tech portfolios, led the group through challenge after challenge, reinforcing his instruction with self-produced, step-by-step videos. Mr. Jaen encouraged participants to jump right in and start to paint and manipulate the sketches they had brought.

There was a triumphant atmosphere in the classroom on the last day, when Mr. Jaen had each person share a rendering showing what had been learned. Any misgivings that digital rendering might cause designers to lose their individuality disappeared during this final presentation. Over 30 students shared their unique and diverse work.[1]

Testimonials: Designer Interviews and Design Galleries

KATHLEEN DONNELLY (FIGURE 8.1–8.2)

I think it would be important for a young designer to know both the art of rendering with paint and paper and the digital process. It is also important in the same vein to have both a paper portfolio and a digital portfolio.

Bio

Kathleen received her MFA in Theatre Design from Northwestern University in Evanston, IL. She moved back to New York and for the next decade designed costumes, lights, and sets for theatre companies and universities in the New York City area. Since the fall of 1995, she has been the resident Costume Designer and Faculty member at UW Oshkosh.

She is currently serving as the Co Vice Commissioner of Expo, Exhibits, and Experience for the USITT Costume Commission. In the past she has served as Chair of the USITT Midwest Regional Section, and is the Past Chair of Design, Technology, and Management for KCACTF Region III.

Interview

Rafael: In your experience, what makes for an effective design collaboration?

Kathleen: An open communication line between all of the team members and a willingness to share ideas as the process develops.

Rafael: What is your role in telling the story?

Kathleen: My role is to help the character tell their story. Additionally, contemporary stage design can sometimes provide only a minimal number of clues to the time period of the play for the audience. It is often the costume designs that frame the time period of the world of the play.

Rafael: What are your thoughts about collaborating with directors, actors, costume technicians, other designers, producers, stage managers, etc.?

Kathleen: I think the key word is collaboration. Directors have clear visions of the world of their creation, and our input is to realize that vision, and along with the other designers create a unified world of the play. The costume technicians are key to the realization of the costume design. My job is to make sure they understand what I am trying to achieve and then work with them to find solutions to the challenges. Stage managers are important to the general communication with the cast and director. They are often the ones in the middle communicating the questions and concerns during rehearsal—your eyes and ears as it were during the rehearsal process.

Rafael: In today's digital era, what are some of the things that you find helpful when communicating with a director and/or production team via the World Wide Web?

Kathleen: In the past three years we have created a Web page for each production and all of the design material, schedules, and daily logs are communicated through this tool. It has not only saved a lot of paper but has also made the information accessible as a tool for students who are just learning the process of production design.

Rafael: What advice would you give a young (or new) practitioner who is starting to work professionally with digital rendering and other Web-sharing platforms?

Kathleen: Practice makes it easier and faster. It is very important to learn the digital tools that are available to make the communication and production process smoother. I think it would be important for a young designer to know both the art of rendering with paint and paper and the digital process. It is also important in the same vein to have both a paper portfolio and a digital portfolio.

Rafael: Are there any additional teaching points or "take aways" that you would like to share?

Kathleen: Have fun and enjoy what you are doing. If you are not enjoying the experience, then you will not be as creative as you can be.

ERIC GRIFFIS (FIGURE 8.3)

The smartphone is an incredible asset! Being able to email or text images of fabric options or costume pieces before purchasing is a great time saver. It's also great to be able to share research images and renderings publicly through Dropbox, Pinterest, or Google Docs so they are readily available in rehearsal or the shop when needed.

FIGURE 8.1

Costume sketch for Alma, *The Christmas Schooner*. By Kathleen Donnelly.

FIGURE 8.2

Group costume sketch for *Antigone*. By Kathleen Donnelly.

Bio

Eric Griffis is the Associate Professor of Costume Design at Georgia College and State University where he has recently designed *Chicago*, *Next Fall*, and *The Piano Lesson* and directed *The Laramie Project*. Other designs include *Billy Elliot* (Ocean State Theatre), *Good Boys and True* (Actor's Express), and *South Pacific* (New London Barn Playhouse). He has also worked at the Costume Craftsperson for the Pennsylvania Shakespeare Festival and Wardrobe for the Alabama Shakespeare Festival. Eric's work can be seen at ericgriffis.com.

Interview

Rafael: In your experience, what makes for an effective design collaboration?

Eric: Communication is key. Take time to understand the various ways in which directors and other designers communicate. While design is a visual field, not everyone communicates well visually. Be prepared to provide additional information through written or spoken words, tactile means, and research. Listening is an often overlooked part of communication. As important as sharing your design concept is taking in the work of other designers and the director and making sure you are on the same page. Listening to actors in fittings is also essential since they know best the physicality of their blocking and choreography.

Rafael: What is your role in telling the story?

Eric: I believe the costumer's role is to tell the story of each character visually while supporting the period and/or world of the play. My approach is to consider what the character would have selected to wear from their wardrobe that particular day.

Rafael: What are your thoughts about collaborating with directors, actors, costume technicians, other designers, producers, stage managers, etc.?

Eric: Collaboration with other artists is the heart of theatre. It is essential to create a cohesive production and a valuable skill outside the world of theatre as well.

Rafael: In today's digital era, what are some of the things that you find helpful when communicating with a director and/or production team via the World Wide Web?

Eric: The smartphone is an incredible asset! Being able to email or text images of fabric options or costume pieces before purchasing is a great time saver. It's also great to be able to share research images and renderings publicly through Dropbox, Pinterest, or Google Docs so they are readily available in rehearsal or the shop when needed. It has also been tremendously helpful as a craftsperson and technician to have this information available when the designer was not around and allowed me to move forward with a project instead of having to wait to have questions answered in person.

Rafael: What advice would you give a young (or new) practitioner who is starting to work professionally with digital rendering and other Web-sharing platforms?

Eric: It can be frustrating, but don't give up. At first, digital rendering may seem like it takes longer than drawing or painting, but once you get the hang of it, it will save you so much time. In order to work with theatres nationwide, abroad, or even multiple shows at one time you must embrace the technology that facilitates that communication and collaboration or you will miss out on opportunities.

FIGURE 8.3

Costume sketch for *Hamlet*. By Eric Griffis.

DEBRA KRAJEC (FIGURE 8.4–8.5)

I think the best experiences for me have been more than 'effective' collaborations. They have been EXCITING collaborations, because everyone at the table feels like the show belongs to us, we have a personal stake in it, and that we have all helped to create this production.

Bio

Debra Krajec is an Associate Professor of Theatre Arts at Marquette University in Milwaukee. Since 1984 she has served as a stage director and costume designer for the Theatre program, and in 2011 she received a John P. Raynor, S.J., Faculty Award for Teaching Excellence. She completed her MFA from Texas Christian University in 1982, and has worked professionally as a costume designer, a director, and an actress. At Marquette, Debra teaches Costume Design, Costume History, History of Period Styles, Stage Directing, and Advanced Stage Directing. Debra has designed costumes for Milwaukee Repertory Theatre, Milwaukee Chamber Theatre, First Stage, Renaissance Theaterworks, Next Act Theatre, Retro Productions, St. Michael's Playhouse, and Casa Mañana Playhouse. She is very active in USITT, where she is a Fellow of the Institute and past Costume Design and Technology Commissioner and Director at Large. She is also a member of the Actors' Equity Association.

Interview

Rafael: In your experience, what makes for effective design collaboration?

Debra: My favorite collaborations have been the ones where EVERYONE shares from day one. The room needs to feel right to have that happen, the vibe has to be there. To me, that means that you get the sense when you walk in the room and put your stuff down, that the others are glad you are there. There is a friendly, welcoming atmosphere, an atmosphere of "Let's talk about this great play—what story do we want to tell? What does it mean to YOU?" Egos are left outside. I think the best experiences for me have been more than "effective" collaborations. They have been EXCITING collaborations, because everyone at the table feels like the show belongs to us, we have a personal stake in it, and that we have all helped to create this production. We have been there at the production's conception and birth, if you know what I mean. We are the lucky ones who get to see it get born and maybe grow up.

Rafael: What is your role in telling the story?

Debra: I think the costumes give the characters real life. Unless you are a practicing naturist, you are going to wear some kind of clothing. And what you choose to wear, or are forced to wear, and how you wear it gives those who look a lot of information about you, maybe about how you are feeling that particular moment, and how you fit in, or not. It's the clothes that inform more than any other design element, in my opinion. They truly are "moving scenery." I still perform from time to time, and when I do, it isn't until I put on my character's shoes that the person is real to me as a performer. Clothes are so very personal. Getting that personal touch right for each character in a play has the power to really make the world of the play come alive with these unique people in it. It's my job to help those actors get inside the skin of the character in a tangible way. The scenery and sound and lights create the characters' world, but the clothing creates THEM. It's my job as a costume designer to get that right, and to help the actor step into the right skin.

Rafael: What are your thoughts about collaborating with directors, actors, costume technicians, other designers, producers, stage managers, etc.?

Debra: I have learned, maybe now that I am older and I have less fear of making a fool of myself, that I don't need to have all the answers. Take the good stuff from wherever it comes. Sometimes the best ideas/thoughts that inform my work come from the sound designer (it seems to me that more and more sound designers have an amazing world view on the play, when I sometimes get stuck in details—I have learned to listen to the sound designer!), or the assistant stage manager, or the intern. Good ideas can come from anybody. I don't have the monopoly on good ideas. Good collaboration comes when everybody feels empowered to share his or her ideas. I love early concept meetings when there is an atmosphere of "There are no bad ideas, let's blue sky this together."

Every costume designer likely has at least one story of collaboration with a scenic designer that didn't go well, when the lines of communication weren't there (see "hoop skirts on a raked stage"). So I have tried harder to get on same page with both scenic and lighting designers early on, and I think it totally pays off. I try to not think that I shouldn't comment on things about the environment, and that they shouldn't offer ideas or thoughts about the clothes. Being territorial does not allow good collaboration. I find it valuable to be as interested in what they are doing with the set and lights as I am in the clothes. Don't just wait your turn to talk. Be present, be interested, and pay attention to what the other designers are saying about the other elements of the production. Share colors; ask questions about flooring and door width, color of wallpaper, quality and color of light. I have learned to ask questions about props, offer help if I can. We all want the same thing—a unified, conceptually appropriate good-looking show. Talking to each other, sharing ideas and information is the only way we are going to get it.

I direct, I perform, and I design—makes me better at all three. I know how to look at a production from all three angles, and it enables me to anticipate needs and prevent problems. I think it might make me more patient. It also helps me to have the specific terminology with which to converse. I also welcome experienced actors' input into their character's appearance—after all, my job is to help them realize their character. I love to hear them talk about their characters, and share their concerns and requests with me. Collaboration with the actor sometimes gets pushed aside, but if I can make an actor more comfortable or feel more in touch with the person they are portraying, and do it within my concept and means, I'll do it. Because nothing looks better on stage than an actor who loves his costume and makes it seem to the audience that his costumes are really his clothes. And if he can do that in Elizabethan pumpkin hose, that's an incredible sight to see.

I love to work with directors who think visually, who can share with words or images their thoughts and feelings about mood or style in a conversation, not a lecture, in a production meeting. The director needs to set the vibe for the type of collaboration the production is going to have. I like directors who ask for opinions, who admit they don't know the answers yet. It seems to me the hardest thing at the beginning for a designer to do is to get on the same wavelength with the director's aesthetic—to figure out what they like and don't like, what to them is a positive or a negative, and to discover if they have a good color sense, if they understand silhouette, if they are responsive to texture and shape and color. Until you understand how they think and figure out the best way to communicate with them, it's a challenge to collaborate. I once worked with a director with no visual sense at all, who didn't know what plaid was, but kept telling me everything needed to be "angular," and that he couldn't tell me what he wanted, but he'd know what was right when he saw it. That was difficult. I love directors who respond to research images or scribbles of ideas on a piece of paper. I really love directors who will scribble with me. My favorite directors I have worked with have been the ones who can talk about what the play means to them, who these people in this world are to them, and might say, "I know this might sound crazy and irrelevant, but this play to me is like ___." You'd be surprised how many times an off-the-wall statement or weird image shared can make everyone in the room go, "OH! Now I get where you're coming from!"

I love to have a good working relationship with everyone involved. Well, duh, of course, who wouldn't? Especially, the people in the costume department. I totally believe that my costumes are only going to be as good as the technicians that build them, so I want to give them as much help, insight, support, love, and chocolate as I can—I want their best work. I need their help. I want them to make suggestions! I know they are very likely to have a better idea how best to build something. I want the costumes to be a collaborative effort with the costume technicians as well. There is nothing better in the whole world than a good draper who understands what you are trying to achieve, and helps you achieve it.

The best stage managers are the ones who understand from the outset that if anything happens in rehearsal that might involve a character's costume, personal choice, movement, or an actor issue, to let me know immediately. Stage managers have headed off some huge problems for me by being an immediate conduit of info. Being in a positive place with the stage manager is vital. Help them and they will help you.

The best collaborations happen when everyone's voice is valued at the table, when the work is respected. It does happen. It's what makes you keep doing this work.

Rafael: In today's digital era, what are some of the things that you find helpful when communicating with a director and/or production team via the World Wide Web?

Debra: I have been designing long enough to remember vividly when the first affordable digital cameras came out and I could take fitting photos and email them to the director—how amazing that was! How much more wonderful the digital tools have become. Dropbox and Box.net are a huge part of my life now. So are Evernote, with its Web clipping function, and Google Drive. All of these file-sharing programs allow you to collaborate digitally on the Internet, post sketches, photographs, research images, spreadsheets, and make comments, even make corrections, and the entire group can see it. Being able to share large image files and get comments back quickly is vital. I am addicted to Pinterest, absolutely addicted! I sometimes use online photo-sharing sites such as Photobucket or Flickr. I always do digital research collages now to share research with directors and other designers. I create them in PowerPoint or Word and post to whatever online file-sharing service is being used for the production, or show them on screen at production meetings. Even when we meet in the hallway or the fitting room, it is great to be able to show images on a tablet or computer, and not have to print everything out and use so much paper and ink. I have used Skype and GoToMeeting and WebEx for long-distance face-to-face meetings (even shopping and fittings sometimes!). I could not survive now without my smartphone and phone camera. Many of the programs I use on my laptop

I have mobile app versions for, and can access information on the road or in costume storage, and send the director or the shop information that they can get immediately, and I can get an answer quickly. Design teams are so often spread out across the country or world these days. Having digital tools, not only for creation of renderings, research boards, and organizational documents, but also for immediate communication, is wonderful.

Rafael: What advice would you give a young (or new) practitioner who is starting to work professionally with digital rendering and other Web-sharing platforms?

Debra:

1. Digital rendering: Since I believe I will always be a beginner when it comes to digital rendering, I would advise anyone new to it to find the way it can work for him or her. By that I mean, it's possible that some parts of digital rendering will work for them, and others seem too labor intensive, but a combination of techniques is not a bad thing. At this point, since I was trained to do my rendering by hand, I still prefer to draw my figures and costumes in pencil on paper the old-fashioned way. But then I tend to do a combination of digital techniques in Photoshop or Painter. I scan my sketches, clean them up, tweak them size and line-color wise, add paint or pattern, put them on interesting backgrounds, collage things in the background, add digital versions of fabric swatches, etc. Sometimes I take them in and out of Photoshop or Painter, adding digital techniques on top of hand-done portions of my rendering. My advice would be to not feel there is a right or wrong way to do it. Use the digital technology to help you with the parts you're comfortable with doing on the computer, or want to learn to do quickly. And never think there is one way to learn about how to render digitally. I have found wonderful instruction not only from Rafael Jaen and Annie Cleveland regarding costume rendering in digital form, but also from digital scrapbooks, fashion illustrators, and photographers. There are wonderful online courses, YouTube videos, and books these days on digital art that can help. Join online groups like Photoshop Training Channel and Phlearn to get regular tips and tutorials emailed to you. And just keep doing it; you have to keep practicing to have the techniques become second nature. Like sketching by hand, the more you do it the easier it will become and the better you will get. There may be a long period of time when you get really frustrated, and it just seems like doing it the old-fashioned way would be faster. For me there still are parts of the process that are faster for me by hand. But I will never stop scanning my sketches, because once they are in digital form, I can make changes, print out multiples and different sizes, send them effortlessly anywhere, in ways that I never ever could have 20 years ago without great trouble and expense. Bottom line—if I can do this, anyone can. Note there will be times of frustration as you learn, but don't give up. Make yourself render a show using Photoshop or Painter. Give yourself extra time to do it. But do it.

2. Web-sharing platforms: I find it interesting that there are still a good number of directors who aren't very computer savvy. That always surprises me, when one is reluctant to go online to look at a Dropbox, or finds it difficult to access. I have had to teach directors how to use the program, and actually that time spent

THE CHERRY ORCHARD

LOPAKHIN

FIGURE 8.4

Costume sketch for Lopakhin, *The Cherry Orchard*. By Debra Krajec.

HOLY DAYS
by Sally Nemeth

ROSIE

FIGURE 8.5

Costume sketch for Rosie, *Holy Days*. By Debra Krajec.

has been totally worth it. I really don't know how I could do what I do without a Web-sharing platform of some sort. Everything would take ten times longer. So my advice would be to get familiar with these different types of platforms. And get accounts of your own. I have been paying for an upgraded subscription to Dropbox and Evernote that enables me to have more storage capacity and ease of functions. It's a business expense that is tax-deductible, and makes my life easier. It is so wonderful to know that all my info is kept in cyberspace in addition to my very vulnerable laptop. My advice is to back up! Back up! Back up! I have important design files backed up in numerous places, just in case. You only have to lose all your materials for a show once in order to see why this is so important. I save show files on my laptop, on Dropbox, and on an external hard drive (and I back up that hard drive to another hard drive) in case I need to access them and do not have a Wi-Fi connection. Perhaps I am paranoid, but it makes me feel more secure!

PATRICIA MARTIN—COSTUME DESIGNER (FIGURE 8.6–8.9)

Digital rendering is not faster or easier than rendering by hand. It is simply another skill that you have in your toolbox.

Bio

Patricia Martin is a professor, vice chair, and head of design for the Department of Theatre at the University of Arkansas, Fayetteville. She has designed costumes for the Southern Theatre Festival, Arkansas Repertory Theatre, TheatreSquared, Idaho Repertory Theatre Idaho Theatre for Youth, the University of Idaho, and Tulsa University. She has also worked professionally in New York as a draper's assistant on a variety of Broadway productions and as a draper for the Colorado Shakespeare Festival and the Utah Shakespearean Festival. She is a member of United Scenic Artists Local 829, a recipient of three ACTF design awards, and served as Costume Design and Technology Commissioner for USITT from 2002–6.

Interview

Rafael: In your experience, what makes for effective design collaboration?

Patricia: The most effective design collaboration happens when everyone is engaged wholeheartedly in the process. The most exciting theatre experiences are created when there is lively discussion, passionate debate, and an overall sense of working together towards a common purpose. Communication is crucial to effective collaboration. We all begin the process with words on a page, then share our ideas, and in a very short time work together to create a complex world that lives on the stage.

Rafael: What is your role in telling the story?

Patricia: I take my role as a storyteller very seriously. The way I tell the story is different from a playwright who uses words or the actor who uses his or her voice, body, emotion, and intellect. I use the language of design through clothing and costume to visual(ly) reinforce character statements, convey those ideas that may not be overtly expressed, reveal secrets that are uncovered, and reinforce the ideas of the playwright and director. The question I always ask myself, as I am making the multitude of choices when designing is, "Am I telling the character's story as clearly and as honestly as I can?" I rely on the actor, the director, and my design colleagues, who are all my collaborators, to provide me with their insight and ideas.

Rafael: What are your thoughts about collaborating with directors, actors, costume technicians, other designers, producers, stage managers, etc.?

Patricia: In my opinion if you want to be a theatre artist you need to be able to work well with others and respect everyone who has committed their effort, time, and talent to the process. Theatre is all about connections—finding a connection to the text, to your theatre colleagues, and ultimately creating a connection to your audience. I find my best collaborations occur when I actively listen and work with everyone involved with the production. When we are all engaged and passionate about the story and the process of creating, collaboration is exciting and incredibly satisfying.

Rafael: In today's digital era, what are some of the things that you find helpful when communicating with a director and/or production team via the World Wide Web?

Patricia: The more that you are confident in your process and the more you share your process with all of your collaborators, the better your communication will be with all of your colleagues.

Rafael: What advice would you give a young (or new) practitioner who is starting to work professionally with digital rendering and other Web-sharing platforms?

Patricia: There are a lot of platforms that you can use to share your work, but I typically provide a PDF version. It is universal and doesn't require any expensive software that the end user has to purchase.

Rafael: Are there any additional teaching points or "take aways" that you would like to share?

Patricia:

- I have also found that typing in notes on the sketch or as part of the presentation has been helpful—especially when a director is not on-site.

- Don't be afraid to mix it up and use both hand drawing and the digital tools available in the software programs to create your work.

- Ask your friends and colleagues for help. There are so many ways to solve problems and most people are more than happy to share their tricks and process.

- Monitor the Web to find tricks and tips.

- Practice and repeat.

- Digital rendering is not faster or easier than rendering by hand. It is simply another skill that you have in your toolbox.

JANE STEIN—COSTUME DESIGNER (FIGURE 8.10)

There is one bus driver and that is the director, everyone else's job is to help, through each individual area, to tell the story that the director wants to tell.

Bio

Jane Alois Stein's costume designs include the Off Broadway productions of *Bill W. and Dr. Bob* for the New World Stages, *Persephone* for BAM (Brooklyn Academy of Music), and Israel Horovitz's *Lebensraum* for the Miranda Theatre. Regional theatre credits include Adam Rapp's *Animals and Plants* for American Repertory Theatre, *A Midsummer Night's Dream* for American Repertory Theatre Institute, *Painting it Red* for Berkeley Repertory, *A Lesson from Aloes* for Repertory Theatre of St. Louis, *Sweeney Todd* for Connecticut Repertory Theatre, *Uncle Broadway* at the Royal George Theatre of

She Stoops to Conquer

Kate Hardcastle

C.D. 10772
COSTUME DESIGNER

FIGURE 8.6

Costume sketch for Kate Hardcastle, *She Stoops to Conquer*. By Patricia Martin.

She Stoops to Conquer

Mr. Hardcastle

C.D. 10772
COSTUME DESIGNER

FIGURE 8.7

Costume sketch for Mr. Hardcastle, *She Stoops to Conquer*. By Patricia Martin.

She Stoops to Conquer

Mrs. Hardcastle

She Stoops to Conquer

Sir Charles Marlow

FIGURE 8.8

Costume sketch for Mrs. Hardcastle, *She Stoops to Conquer*. By Patricia Martin.

FIGURE 8.9

Costume sketch for Sir Charles Marlow, *She Stoops to Conquer*. By Patricia Martin.

Chicago, and *King Lear* for New Repertory Theatre. Work at other theatres includes designs for American Stage Festival, Bloomsburg Theatre Ensemble, Commonwealth Shakespeare, Gloucester Stage Company, Merrimack Repertory Theatre, North Shore Music Theatre, and Theatre by the Sea. Opera productions include designs for the Opera Theatre of St. Louis and the Boston Musica Viva. For television Jane designed the wardrobe of Russell Baker for WGBH Masterpiece Theatre. Jane is the head of Costume Design/Technology for the theatre department of Virginia Tech. Previously she taught Scenic and Costume Design at Wheaton College for 12 years. She is a member of United Scenic Artists Local 829, USITT, and the Costume Society of America.

Interview

Rafael: In your experience, what makes for effective design collaboration?

Jane: I think in order to be an effective design collaborator, you have to be a team player. Egos must be left at the door. There is one bus driver and that is the director; everyone else's job is to help, through each individual area, to tell the story that the director wants to tell. As a costume designer, I would be doing myself a disservice by ignoring the other designers and what they have to contribute to the production. It is not about being told what to do, but rather bringing your ideas to the table to help bring about a cohesive production on this wild ride of storytelling that we do.

Rafael: What is your role in telling the story?

Jane: My job is to help, through the choices I make in costume pieces, tell the story of the characters in the play that I am designing. This is true of all the characters, not just the main ones. The audience

has a short amount of time to get to know these people, so whatever I can do to help them will only add to their experience of seeing the show. It's about making truthful decisions, and not those that are arbitrary.

Rafael: What are your thoughts about collaborating with directors, actors, costume technicians, other designers, producers, stage managers, etc.?

Jane: The more you can collaborate, and communicate with everyone involved, the more effective the production. If you can have a discussion with an actor about their character, and gain insight of who they think it is, this information can only help you. There is nothing more frustrating than designing a costume for a character that you think is one way, and see an actor portray them the exact opposite. Which is also why you want those types of conversations with the director. As for the other designers—well, who hasn't had your costumes turned to mud on stage, because you didn't have conversations with the lighting designer? Or had a costume disappear on stage, because the wall color and the costume are the exact same color? Producers want to know that you are a team player, and helping bring a cohesive production to fruition. It's their money, and they should be kept in the loop. Stage managers! They are your eyes and ears in the rehearsal process. If they don't know what you are planning, they cannot help you. So, how do you know that the tight straight skirt you designed for character A isn't going to work, because she enters the stage doing cartwheels? Costume technicians— you had better talk to these people! Without them, the most fantastic designs are nothing but lines on paper. Everyone working on your designs will be much more invested if they understand the ride that you went on to get to the final step. I love talking to drapers/cutters about where that seam should be, or how they think something should be rigged for a quick change. The more involved the entire shop is, the more invested they are!

Rafael: In today's digital era, what are some of the things that you find helpful when communicating with a director and/or production team via the World Wide Web?

Jane: Oh, my! How much easier is it to work on the same production when everyone is in a different part of the country or world? Prior to the digital age, we all had to free up days to have everyone meet in one place. There was always that one person who could not physically make the meeting, so the best you could do is have them on the phone with not very clear copies of renderings or ground plans. Now with things like Dropbox, we can all be looking at the exact same things while being miles apart. Having said that, I do still think at least one meeting with everyone in the same room is wonderful, as I enjoy actually meeting and seeing people in the flesh. But that is not always possible.

Rafael: What advice would you give a young (or new) practitioner who is starting to work professionally with digital rendering and other Web-sharing platforms?

Jane: Practice, practice, practice! I have had students who think that you somehow become a better artist by going digital. I tell them, the computer doesn't draw it for you. You still need to be able to draw on your own. The computer is a fabulous device when you need to change something about your design, as you don't need to necessarily start over from scratch. Instead you can go to that layer and delete the color or the line. You save a lot of time by just changing something, rather than completely starting over. You still need all the tools of design. The computer doesn't think for you . . . at least not yet.

Rafael: Are there any additional teaching points or "take aways" that you would like to share?

Jane: As someone who was not raised with a computer in my hand, as so many of my students are these days, I went into the whole digital thing kicking and screaming. I hated the idea of all of it! Now, much to my chagrin, I can't imagine a world of design and theatre without it.

ESTHER VAN EEK—COSTUME DESIGNER (FIGURE 8.11)

Curiosity and critique are essential to good design. Curiosity motivates learning and critique builds discernment.

Bio

Esther Van Eek works in theatre and visual art primarily as a costume designer and printmaker. A member of Associated Designers of Canada, she holds a BFA in Printmaking and an MFA in Production Design. She is passionate about research, re-purposing garments, and manipulating surfaces with various treatments including painting and block printing. She teaches for the School of Dramatic Art at the University of Windsor, and serves as faculty costume designer for the University Players. She has worked in the United States and Canada designing costumes, millinery, props, and sets. Her design work has won several awards from the KC-ACTF, and she is an active member of USITT and CITT. Her professional credits include designs for the Academy of Classical Acting, the Shakespeare Theatre, Studio Theatre, and Didactic Theatre. Her recent work for Shakespeare & Company includes designs for *Parasite Drag* and *The Taming*.

The Servant of two Masters

Smeraldina

jane alois stein

Interview

Rafael: In your experience, what makes for effective design collaboration?

Esther: The best experiences I've had as a designer involved clear communication—early and often—with everyone involved on a project. This builds an environment of trust and mutual respect in which creativity thrives.

Rafael: What is your role in telling the story?

Esther: By repeated careful readings of the script, I glean information about the world the playwright has created and the characters that populate it. Thoughtfully designed costumes will give the audience visual clues to that world and its culture, and to each character's personality, belief system, relationships, and place within that world. In providing these clues, the costume becomes an essential tool for the actor and a key element to conveying the story.

Rafael: What are your thoughts about collaborating with directors, actors, costume technicians, other designers, producers, stage managers, etc.?

Esther: I most enjoy creative collaborations where each member of the team is expected to bring their best to the table, when ideas flow, meld, and evolve so, finally, it is not a series of good ideas anymore, but a dynamic, unified telling of the story.

Rafael: In today's digital era, what are some of the things that you find helpful when communicating with a director and/or production team via the World Wide Web?

Esther: I find that on most of my projects, a shared folder in Dropbox provides an easy, efficient way to share research and sketches, and to see what the other members of the team are thinking. When you're often not in the same city, or even same time zone, this is a great way to keep the conversation going.

Rafael: What advice would you give a young (or new) practitioner who is starting to work professionally with digital rendering and other Web-sharing platforms?

Esther: These tools have become part of the design landscape and young practitioners seem to have an innate understanding of them. My advice is to keep up a traditional drawing—especially figure drawing—practice as well, so whatever the tools used, the resulting designs are expressive and celebrate your creative mark.

Rafael: Are there any additional teaching points or "take aways" that you would like to share?

Esther: Curiosity and critique are essential to good design. Curiosity motivates learning and critique builds discernment. Strive to stay open to both in your artistic practice.

KATHRYN WAGNER—COSTUME DESIGNER (FIGURE 8.12–8.13)

I need to be supportive of the actor and their choices for the character as well as keeping hold of my own vision for the production.

Bio

Kathryn Wagner is currently an Associate Professor of Costume Design and Head of Design and Technical Production at Western Michigan University. Prior to working at WMU, Ms. Wagner taught at Southern Illinois University and Oakland University. She has designed for Hope Summer Repertory Theatre, Michigan Shakespeare Festival, the Peninsula Players, University of Illinois Summerfest, McLeod Summer Playhouse, Meadow Brook Theatre, Sullivan's Little Theater on the Square, AMAS Musical Theatre, New Jersey Shakespeare

CRIMES OF THE HEART
by Beth Henley
Directed by Liza Balkan
Costume Design by Esther Van Eek

FIGURE 8.11

Costume sketch for Barnette, *Crimes of the Heart.* By Esther Van Eek.

Festival, McCarter Theatre, and the Lamb's Theatre Company. In addition, she worked for Mulder/Martin Inc., where she was involved in the making of many corporate and sports mascots, puppet characters, and a variety of walking corporate logos. Ms. Wagner holds a BFA from DePaul University, Goodman School of Drama and an MFA from Rutgers University, Mason Gross School of the Arts. Ms. Wagner is a member of the Costume Society of America, USITT, and United Scenic Artists Local 829.

Interview

Rafael: In your experience, what makes for effective design collaboration?

Kathryn: An effective collaboration involves all areas coming together to create a cohesive production that supports the story and the production as a whole. It is always great when ideas for a design come from the conversations that the designers and directors have together.

Rafael: What is your role in telling the story?

Kathryn: My role as a costume designer is to aid the actors in bringing their characters to life. I feel strongly that as the costume designer, I need to be supportive of the actor and their choices for the character as well as keeping hold of my own vision for the production.

Rafael: What are your thoughts about collaborating with directors, actors, costume technicians, other designers, producers, stage managers, etc.?

Kathryn: I prefer for all areas to work together in the design of the show. It is always a bit disappointing to work with a director who wants to just dictate the entire look of the show and the designers simply become facilitators and/or coordinators for the project. As a costume designer, my work with

actors is a total collaboration and I feel strongly that the designs work well for them as they are portraying the character on the stage. Collaborating with costume technicians is extremely important, as they are the ones who take the design off the 2D rendering and re-create it in 3D on the actor. It is important to work with all of the various areas of the production, as we are all working towards the same common goal.

Rafael: In today's digital era, what are some of the things that you find helpful when communicating with a director and/or production team via the World Wide Web?

Kathryn: It is extremely easy now to communicate your research and designs to others through the Web. In a world where you may be designing or working in locations all over the country, design and production meetings can now easily be held without having to travel to those locations. I have attended meetings via Skype, FaceTime, and through GoToMeeting. I have found it helpful to utilize more than one computer device during these meetings—one to communicate with, the other to be able to access the Internet, your own research, Dropbox, etc. This allows you to quickly add things into the discussion.

Rafael: What advice would you give a young (or new) practitioner who is starting to work professionally with digital rendering and other Web-sharing platforms?

Kathryn: Photoshop and other CAD programs are a communication tool—simply another way to communicate with fellow designers and technicians. Use the digital tools to help get your ideas across, but do not abandon the hand tools—drawing and painting, model building, etc. You still need to be able to quickly draw something out or make changes in the shops where you may not have access to your computer.

FIGURE 8.12

Costume sketch for Cervantes as Don Quixote, *Man of La Mancha*. By Kathryn Wagner.

FIGURE 8.13

Costume sketch for The Dynamites, *Hairspray*. By Kathryn Wagner.

WENDI R. ZEA—COSTUME DESIGNER (FIGURE 8.14)

Finding a way to bring multiple viewpoints on a production together can be challenging, but also exhilarating.

Bio

Wendi R. Zea is an Associate Professor in Costume Design at Southern Illinois University, and teaches design, period styles, costumes construction, play reading, and a variety of costume crafts classes, including dyeing, fabric modification, wigs, and millinery. She has designed costumes for numerous professional theatres including Cortland Repertory Theatre (where her design for *1776* won a regional award), Porthouse Theatre, Northern Stage, and McLeod Summer Playhouse. At SIU, Wendi has designed many productions, including *Cosi Fan Tutte* and *Irving Berlin's White Christmas*. Her design work has been presented at the United States Institute for Theatre Technology Conference Design Expo, and she has done presentations at USITT and SETC on the benefits of using half-scale dress forms as teaching aids. Her major research areas include using computer rendering techniques, costume history, and color theory.

Interview

Rafael: In your experience, what makes for effective design collaboration?

Wendy: An effective design collaboration begins with the designers and director discussing the play together, sharing the vision and exploring ideas about the story and characters before jumping straight to the practical.

Rafael: What is your role in telling the story?

Wendy: As costume designer, my role in telling the story is to help the audience know who these characters are—what they want, how they live, their function in the story—and track the evolution of the character through what they wear. The costume designer reinforces the story visually that the actors are telling verbally.

Rafael: What are your thoughts about collaborating with directors, actors, costume technicians, other designers, producers, stage managers, etc.?

Wendy: I love working with other members of the production. Finding a way to bring multiple viewpoints on a production together can be challenging, but also exhilarating. Seeing the work through the eyes of your colleagues can be extremely helpful in refining your own ideas.

Rafael: In today's digital era, what are some of the things that you find helpful when communicating with a director and/or production team via the World Wide Web?

Wendy: The most helpful to me has been using any of the various platforms (Dropbox, Box, OneNote) to share images and other information with the rest of the design team. Having it all in one location, instead of wading through multiple emails, makes sharing and responding to each other much easier.

Rafael: What advice would you give a young (or new) practitioner who is starting to work professionally with digital rendering and other Web-sharing platforms?

Wendy: Continue to practice and expand your rendering skills, and be able to work both digitally and by hand—each will improve the other. And become familiar with multiple Web-sharing platforms, as different theatres will utilize different ones.

Rafael: Are there any additional teaching points or "take aways" that you would like to share?

FIGURE 8.14

Costume sketch for The Devils, Igor Stravinsky's *The Soldier's Tale*. By Wendi R. Zea.

Wendy: Continue to explore new methods of communicating, both through your renderings and your designs. Twice now I have used a technique that has proven very successful: after gaining the set designer's permission, I will add my digital renderings to a digital copy of their set rendering. This allows the director to get a clearer picture of how the two will work together, from scene to scene, and get a good view of the show as a whole.

Final Words

As a practicing 21st-century designer, I find that it is important to combine one's classical training with the use of digital applications. This alleviates the competing demands in today's work field. I regularly combine Google Docs, Pinterest, Photoshop, Dropbox folders, Flickr archives, iPhone apps, etc. to help tackle the design process "on the go." I have been fortunate enough to present my findings at various PDWs and costume symposiums, and at multiple colleges around the USA. I have also taught successful online courses. I've specially focused in producing sketches using

Photoshop, so I can save them as PDF files and email them without using scanners, printers, watercolor paper, etc. The software allows me to translate basic principles of traditional media. I can create watercolor transparency and acrylic opacity in digital renderings full of substance and intent. In addition, the engineering behind it provides me with a painting desk-station that I can use anywhere—making fast design changes with no fuss.

Thank you for joining me in rediscovering the excitement and passion that motivate costume designers. Let's get inspired and try all (or some) of the digital approaches described in this book.

Citations and Sources

1   Van Eek, Esther. "An Unforgettable Affair with Photoshop." October 2010. Accessed August 29, 2016. http://sightlines.usitt.org/archive/2011/10/CostumeSymposium.asp.